No Ordinary American

No Ordinary American

My Father's Story

Esther E. Hansen

BALBOA.
PRESS
A DIVISION OF HAY HOUSE

Balboa Press books may be ordered through booksellers or by contacting:

Balboa Press
A Division of Hay House
1663 Liberty Drive
Bloomington, IN 47403
www.balboapress.com
1 (877) 407-4847

Because of the dynamic nature of the Internet, any web addresses or links contained in this book may have changed since publication and may no longer be valid. The views expressed in this work are solely those of the author and do not necessarily reflect the views of the publisher, and the publisher hereby disclaims any responsibility for them.

The author of this book does not dispense medical advice or prescribe the use of any technique as a form of treatment for physical, emotional, or medical problems without the advice of a physician, either directly or indirectly. The intent of the author is only to offer information of a general nature to help you in your quest for emotional and spiritual well-being. In the event you use any of the information in this book for yourself, which is your constitutional right, the author and the publisher assume no responsibility for your actions.

Any people depicted in stock imagery provided by Thinkstock are models, and such images are being used for illustrative purposes only.
Certain stock imagery © Thinkstock.

Print information available on the last page.

ISBN: 978-1-5043-3259-0 (sc)
ISBN: 978-1-5043-3260-6 (e)

Balboa Press rev. date: 06/10/2015

Acknowledgement

With deep gratitude I acknowledge the trust and support of my friends. They have contributed in various measure to the creation of this book. Without them it could not have become a reality.

Introduction

My father was an immigrant to the United States of America. He was 21 years old when he came to this country from Denmark. It was 1907 – a year after the earthquake that had devastated San Francisco.

San Francisco welcomed those who were prepared to forget the past, build a new city, a new future. For the young man who would one day become my father, it was an exciting prospect – a new life!

In his memoirs Paul E. Hansen shared many of the adventures that filled the years before and after he became an American citizen. His writings have become mine to share on a larger scale. Many are included here in direct quotation, along with my own recollections of the stories he told and my own impressions of the father I knew, lived with and loved.

He was part of my life. I knew him to be no ordinary American.

Table of Contents

New Life

New Land -New Life

"That's it!" "There it is!" He was among the first to spot the famous landmark. The Statue of Liberty! Real and actual!

Paul E. Hansen could hardly be classified as belonging to the "huddled masses" seeking freedom on the American continent. He was neither tired nor poor. "Full of vim and vigor" would have been a more apt description. He was well dressed in the clothes handmade for him by his mother. And he even had a few American paper dollars helpfully provided by his family before he left Denmark and tucked under the lining of his shoes. At 21 he was well prepared for adventure and experience – a new life in a new land.

It had been a rough, stormy ten-day journey from Denmark across the great ocean to the USA. March is no friendly month for shipboard travelers crossing the Atlantic. But like all Scandinavians, the young traveler was accustomed to the salty ocean air and the rolling deck under his feet; he had "sea legs". But it was time to find more stable footing. Like the others on board the Norwegian "SSHellig Olav" he was glad to spot the arm of the Statue of Liberty, raised in welcome to the new immigrants.

He joined with those who boarded a small boat that ferried them to Ellis Island – the important first stop where they would be officially recorded as new immigrants to the United States of America. The papers he fingered in his pocket were all in order; he was ready to speak his first words of English in response to the questions he would be asked. That done, it was on to Manhattan, the first solid land of the new and exciting world that lay before him.

Paul had noticed two men sitting on a bench near the dock. He approached them now and shouted a question: "How do you get to San Francisco?" Only later did it occur to him, with a chuckle, that he had spoken Danish, and that the men had responded in the same language. They were ready for a chat.

"Hvor kommer du fra i Danmark?" Wherever they were in the world, it was the first question Danes always asked of each other. "Where do you come from in Denmark?" So they plied the young man with questions, and soon found out that he came from Koge, the seaport town familiar to all Danes, only 39 kilometers southwest of Copenhagen.

They learned that his father owned the Hotel Norske Love (The Norwegian Lion), that he had a number of siblings, one of whom had already established himself as a successful carpenter and contractor in San Francisco. Two sisters, he said, both had plans to join him there.

"What can you do?" "Not much. I was a grocery store apprentice in Denmark. But I can do whatever I need to do to make a living."

At long last they answered Paul's first question. "San Francisco is that way." They pointed west. "and it's 3200 miles if you're walking. It's 3000 miles by train, and the fare to San Francisco is 38 dollars. Do you have money? - Well, good! Okay. Then you're all set. Goodby, then, --and have a good trip! Lykke paa rejsen!"

Paul didn't waste a minute. He was quick to find his way to Grand Central Station, where he paid the 38 dollars for his ticket to San Francisco, coach all the way. "That will be easy for a young fellow like you," some Americans on the ship had told him. By late afternoon on the same day he arrived in New York, he was westward bound.

There was a dining car, but his funds were insufficient for meals there. When the train made a brief stop he jumped out, ran to a grocery store and supplied himself with bread and cheese, lunch meat and fruit. Later, on his first night in the USA, he slept soundly in his coach seat all the way to Chicago.

On arrival in the big city he had to board a different train for San Francisco. He could have waited for special transportation designed to facilitate the transfer, but the explanations about that were beyond his grasp of American English. Instead he set off briskly on foot and eventually found the other station.

The train did not leave until 6 P.M., so he checked his two suitcases and decided to see whatever there was to see in the city of Chicago. --Not much, apparently, for a pedestrian cautious of losing his way on the unfamiliar city streets and missing his train connection. But he found a fine little restaurant where he had a good meal for 75 cents.

In good time he was back at the railway station, where he located the train that would take him west to San Francisco. It pulled out promptly at 6 P.M.. Sleeping cars and dining cars were available for folks who had the necessary cash. Paul found a good place in a third class coach, not over the wheels this time, but comfortably in the center, where he'd have smooth sailing, day and night. He slept undisturbed and had a wonderful time on board the train for the next four days.

Paul also soon found the cheapest way to get his meals en route. The train made many regular stops at small stations along the way. The conductor would call out the duration of the stay, usually about 15 minutes, or as much as half an hour. As the train slowed down and came to a stop, the immigrants stood ready at the doors to pile out and charge across the tracks in a quick dash to the nearest saloon.

"What's this all about?" Paul was quick to understand. Customers who purchased a beer were given "all you can eat" for their five cent payment. This was customary procedure in all the small towns between Chicago and San Francisco, wherever the train had a brief layover.

This suited Paul just fine. He was soon among the first to make it to the saloon, and among the last who made it back, just in time, with a mug of beer in one hand and a sandwich in the other. Only one thing puzzled him. As he dashed back to the train he saw men hanging out the windows and shouting. "He's going to make it! Here he comes!" He hadn't understood the words at first. Finally he asked the conductor. "Do they mean me?"

"That's it," the man replied. "They've got bets on whether or not you'll make it back in time to the train."

"And if I don't make it back in time?"

"You'll have to wait for the next train."

"And when would that be?"

"Same time tomorrow."

Those who bet on his not making it back before the train pulled off never won.

At 5 A.M. on the morning before they reached San Francisco, Paul was awakened by the conductor. "Come on, we've got a stop shortly. You're coming to breakfast with me, the engineer and the brakeman."

The four men settled at a table in a small restaurant near the tracks. It was a good breakfast of orange juice, coffee, ham and eggs, and rolls. Paul assured them that he would pay. "Oh, no, this one's on us!" And the three men disclosed what had happened on the trip. To avert suspicion, they had engaged a man to take the bets on whether their young friend would make it back to the train on time after his quick trip to the saloon. Needless to say it was easy for them to assure that the train never pulled out without Paul Hansen on board. Each of the men had made a hundred dollars on the bets. That's why they had invited Paul to breakfast. Now the table rocked with their laughter. And Paul tucked the two dollars he had ready back into his pocket.

That same day the train pulled into Oakland, then on by ferry to the city that was fast rising from the ruins it wanted to forget. One year after the devastating earthquake and the disastrous fire that followed it, San Francisco was already regaining recognition as the "golden gate" beside the Pacific.

It had been a memorable cross-country trip. Paul wrote home enthusiastically about all the "fine folks" he met on the train. He loved them all and many of them would long remember that "nice young fellow from Denmark" who was always ready for a long chat, quick with a kind word or a hearty laugh. "It got so," Paul later wrote in his memoirs, "I didn't care if we never got to San Francisco. I had a good time and loved everyone aboard the train."

There were several good offers of jobs in California, but he turned them down. He wanted time to explore, get acquainted, locate his brother Walter, and make his own way in this exciting new world. A couple from New York inquired about where their young friend planned to stay in San Francisco. Well, he said, a brother of his had settled here, but he'd have to locate him, he'd lost the address. "Come and stay with us," they responded, "until you get settled."

He was glad to accept the offer, and spent his first night in San Francisco as a guest at the Palace Hotel, which had been hastily reconstructed, for a brief sojourn as the "Baby Palace" after the earthquake of 1906. Officialdom in San Francisco was quick to silence discussion of that disaster and the subsequent details of the horrific fire that followed. The major resurrection of the Palace in its previous luxurious splendor was welcomed in 1909. After breakfast the next morning Paul was eager to be on his way. "You'll always be welcome to visit us in New York," said his new friends, "if you ever go back there." The morning fog had lifted. After parking his suitcases their guest strode off into the morning sunlight. It was April 1907 and Paul Hansen was about to become a resident of San Francisco.

San Francisco Here I Am!

It was easy to inquire about Walter Hansen at the many restaurants and saloons he found on his way. He soon ran into someone who knew his brother well. "He lives on De Haro Street in the Mission District," the man said. Paul fetched his suitcases from the Palace Hotel and moved into a small hotel nearby where the rent was $2.50 per week. He wanted to be sure he had a place to stay if Walter was not at home.

But there he was when Paul came back that evening. Walter was a bachelor; he had already built some houses on De Haro Street and lived in one of them. They talked about the family back in Denmark, and Paul was introduced to one of the neighbors. Did he want to work as a carpenter? Paul had never done that but he was willing to try. He went off with an address in his pocket and planned to go there the next morning.

Here's what he had to say about his first job in California:

> *The next day I went to work as a carpenter's helper: two dollars per day, 9-hour-day, 6 day-week. I lasted a full day before I was fired. The foreman told me that as a carpenter I would make a good grocery clerk. I don't know whether my brother told him, but that's exactly what I had been in Denmark. (After four years of apprentice work in a grocery store, pay would begin.)*

The next day he had a job on Guerrero Street in a grocery store. Here's what Paul had to tell about his second job:

> *The boss told me what I had to do. At 9A.M. we got a horse and buggy from the back of the building and I started out to take orders from the customers who didn't come to the store themselves. The boss told me that the horse knew where to stop and so he did. Only he knew he had a new driver and it wasn't long before he stopped at every house on the street and on nearby streets as well. By 12 o'clock he decided to turn homewards, where I found the boss had been out looking for us. Both I and the horse got a talking to: too many wrong houses, too many orders.—Well, I lasted in my second job a week. The grocer told me I'd better look for another one.*

Landing a new job here was no problem. As he moved around San Francisco, Paul was all eyes. Everywhere there was activity The city was alive with construction workers and the impressive results of their labors as new structures went up. It was hard to believe that only a year before 80 percent of the city was in total ruin, that over 3000 people had perished in the earthquake and the terrible fire that ensued. San Francisco was returning to new and vigorous life. resuming its role on the west coast as queen of the Pacific. Ships bearing the American flag would soon depart again from the Golden Gate.

On Tuesday morning Paul was at work again, this time at Union Iron Works, a shipbuilding yard. It was hard, hot work, making nuts and bolts in front of an open fire. The workers were paid $10.90 for a six-day week, nine hours per day. It was not long before he learned that a strike was intended. Everybody went off, some 7 or 8000 men He didn't mind joining the strikers.

Through my friend Mr. Reed. Who had helped me get the job, I was introduced to some of the labor leaders; they asked me if I could speak "union talk" and if I could get around "Frisco" making speeches in various languages, for there were people of many nationalities among the workers. I was told what to say and given the words in five different languages: English, French, German, Spanish and Polish. I memorized the words and then went off to get police permission to hold public meetings at several different places

The first meeting was at Third and Market streets. There were a couple of thousand people there. I spoke for about an hour and a half. The crowd was excited. They cheered and clapped.

After the speech, a gentleman came up to me and introduced himself as Eugene Debs, the socialist candidate for president of the United States. "Son," he said, "I'd like to ask you something. You've talked all this time. I haven't understood a word. But there are well over a thousand people here and everybody applauded. What were you talking about and why were they all so enthusiastic?"

I told him, "I speak Polish and mention <u>more money, less work</u> The Poles like that; they clap their hands and so do all the other people. I do the same in German, then in French, then in Spanish. Then I speak Danish and a little American -- you see?" He did.

Mr. Debs was a gentleman; he treated me to oysters and beer after the crowd dispersed. He wanted me to come with him on his campaign trip, but I refused the

> *offer. "When we have won this strike": (which we did) I said, "I'm going to southern California for a vacation, maybe. Work? Could be."*

Paul did not know that the friendly man who had just treated him was the best known socialist in the United States. Eugene Debs ran for the American presidency five times, one of them in 1908. He was himself a fine orator, so he soon recognized a good speaker when he heard one.

When he tired of speaking, Paul went around San Francisco, just taking everything in. There was plenty to see and a lot to learn. It seemed like a miracle that the earthquake and fire had devastated the city only a year before. These energetic, cheerful folk had certainly been active. He was learning to love "Frisco" and its wonderful people.

Home Base – San Francisco

Whenever Paul scheduled a vacation somewhere in California, or the surrounding areas, it was no problem for him to find a job in San Francisco on his return. He could take his pick of an unending array of jobs. The nearest possibility might be no more than a quick walk ahead of him down the street. He just had to keep an eye out for whatever might come catapulting in his way It might be another goal-bent man on foot, a horse-drawn buggy or wagon, a bicycle, a tin lizzie -there were already lots of those- and, of course streetcars going every which way. There were no traffic rules to control whatever might be found on the main thoroughfares through the rapidly developing city.

One of the places in which Paul enjoyed working was a small restaurant with a very limited menu. Only two items were sold, hamburgers and corned beef. The place was owned by a Dane and was doing a tremendous business -- never closed. Three crews were kept busy 24 hours a day on 8-hour shifts.,

There were a great many Danes in the city, and they were a fine lot. They invited us to their homes for dinner and for parties. Walter introduced me to his many friends and I became a member of two clubs. There were three Danish clubs in town. One of them was quite high class. They didn't give any dances. The Danish Brotherhood was a very large club; almost everyone of Danish descent belonged to that one. They gave you a bonus of $1000 when you died. Besides that one I joined another one called Helga. I liked it a lot and they gave you a thousand dollars worth of fun and dancing before you passed away. Lots of parties, lots of dances, but girls –three boys for every girl.

I didn't enjoy taking girls home, always had to hire a horse and buggy and never got home till 5 or 6A.M. when I had to return the horse. We'd get to the girl's house, she'd just jump out. "Good night and thank you," she'd say. There we were, the horse and I. It got so I'd call every horse "Sourpuss". They always seemed to give me the ha-ha's when a girl said "Good night and thank you." "Some day I'll give you the ha-ha's," said I to the horse

There must have been a song about the three Danish clubs. I heard it some years later as a member of the American Expeditionary Forces in France. But that's another story

Paul's brother Walter had earned a great deal of money helping to repair and replace buildings in the devastated golden gate city. Profits from the sale of a new house he had built recently padded his bank account. He was ready for a new venture. -- What would it be?

There had been a lot of talk about Petaluma—close enough to have felt the effects of the quake, but relatively unharmed. River boats made for easy access to and from the two cities. Petaluma was becoming known for chicken processing, was called "the egg capital of the world." Walter had married a Norwegian girl; together the two of them scouted the area and talked about starting a chicken farm. They picked one out, just three miles from Petaluma.

How would Paul like to be a farmer, own a chicken ranch and fruit farm? Well, Walter's brother Paul didn't think much of the idea, but he went along with it. Together they drove out to the farm, just to check out what he thought of the place and whether he would like farm life. It was a fine place, 10 acres (4 in fruit), a four-room house, partly furnished, barn, one horse, a buggy, a cow, chicken houses, 300 chickens, and some 400 small chicks, only a few weeks old. In the kitchen was a bucket of water, which we tasted. The agent emphasized how good the water was there.

> *Walter borrowed money from a bank and some friend. I put up $500, a lot of money in those days. The people who owned the place wanted cash. The man had died, and his widow wanted to go back to her parents in Ohio. We paid $2800.*
>
> *The first thing we had to do was to dig a well and build a platform for a pump. We had found out that the only water on the place was in that bucket in the kitchen. Every day the agent had put a bucket of water there. While we were there Old Sourpuss, the horse, took me to the dances in Petaluma on Saturday nights. – Three miles there and three miles back, home at 11P.M. He didn't care if I was awake or asleep; he knew his way home.*
>
> *We had good neighbors and life on the farm was all right but dull. We made $700 during our stay there, but six months after our arrival we had had it. We sold the farm and everything on it for $3500 and went back to San Francisco. Neither of us ever again became farmers or tried to raise chickens*

Back in 'Frisco the brothers went their separate ways. Walter was interested in an automobile; there were lots of them on the streets by then. He bought a "tin lizzie" and was well satisfied with the purchase. For a while he made his car a "jitney" (taxicab), but he lost interest in that. Soon he went back to carpentering; by and by he became a contractor.

Paul had his eye on owning a restaurant. With that in view He put $1200 in the bank. It made sense, but it turned out to be a mistake. On Friday night of the week he made his deposit, the cashier at the bank absconded with $ 200,000 and made off for South America. The bank went bankrupt, and Paul's dreams of a nice little restaurant also took wing. What to do? – Try something new!

I got a job as a muleskinner in northern California, where I drove a stagecoach from a railway station to a hotel some 50 miles up in the mountains. I got along fine, though it was sometimes hard, and taking care of the mules was quite a job. Yet I liked the outdoor life and the mountains. The passengers on the stage, mostly well-to-do people, were usually nice and friendly. I had some fun with some of them, telling them about some wonderful "springs" they ought to visit – only a ten minute walk from the hotel.

I guess most of them enjoyed telling about this little adventure when they got back home. Nobody said anything though, until one day I had spoken about the springs to two ladies. They went there, got real angry about it, and told the manager off. The thing was I had placed four old bed springs in a deep hole and put a cover over it. When someone lifted the cover and found only four iron springs, he or she might get a little disappointed, but could see the joke. I had never said they would find water, just called it "four iron springs". Well, the two ladies got sore, the manager got real mad, and I lost a job.

Back I went to San Francisco and to my little hotel named "Dania", off Third, near Howard. Mostly Scandinavians lived there. In our off hours we would play poker, someone would go out for beer and hamburgers. Easy living, and no worries!

One of those who had joined the poker players at the Dania was a big, heavy-set man who looked old but was actually only 35. Spike, as they called him, worked in a nearby restaurant as a dishwasher 26 days a month. On the last of those days, regular as clockwork, the same gentleman would show up at the Dania, looking for Spike. If he was with the other fellows he'd go out in the hall to meet with the man. Then, without saying a word, he'd come back and sit down to play cards with the rest of the men. That evening would be the last they saw of Spike for four days. He went out the next day all dressed up in his one and only good suit, stopped at the bank and cashed a check for one thousand dollars. Then he proceeded up Kearny Street to Barbary Coast and his prostitute friends.

Once Spike invited me to go along with him. I did, but it was too much for me; I left after three days. Eat, drink and be merry 20 hours a day, then 4 hours sleep! We always wondered how he could stand it, but he did, and would be back washing dishes again for 26 days.

I had known Spike for about six months when I heard that He had been found dead in some prostitute's room after one of his sprees. I asked the boys in the hotel if anyone was going to the graveside ceremony. My roommate wouldn't go, but another young fellow my age went along. The two of us took the car (electric cars in those days) and got to San Mateo in plenty of time.

At the cemetery, besides us two, there was only a man we didn't know, and, of course, someone from the funeral home. No prayer or talk was allowed.

After the ceremony, we went across the road for a beer, waiting for the car to take us back to San Francisco. The man we had seen at the grave followed us and asked if we had been friends of Spike for a long time. He was not really interested, he was just making talk and we ignored him.

Just before he left he spoke to us again. Did we want to know who he was? No, we didn't care. Spike was dead now, that's all there was to it. "Well, he said, "I was his lawyer and in his will he stated that I was to turn over to anyone attending his funeral $250. He had expected some of his girl friends, but you two are the only ones here." He gave us each $250 in gold, turned and left. So did we – richer, but not sad. Spike was better off dead, we thought.

San Francisco

1906-1915

The Great Outdoors

Adventures with Fred

Paul was never slow to make friends. He joined a Danish club where it felt good to revert to his native tongue. There were always those who shared his love of hiking.

Fred was the cook in the boarding house where Paul was living, close to the Union Iron Works on Potreo Street. The two were about the same age and became good friends

Fred was from Riverside in the mountains east of Los Angeles. His father owned a large orange grove and the family had a fine home there. Fred and his older brothers had grown up close to nature, with lots of camping, hunting and fishing in the mountains.

The two buddies planned a vacation trip, beginning in southern California. With almost fifty dollars in his pocket in gold and silver, Paul felt ready to deal with any expenses they might encounter on the way.

In those days there was no paper money in California; it was the time of the "depression" of 1907. Workers were paid their wages in certificates, which some people were willing to accept as money. The saloons would give gold or silver for the certificates if the customer would buy two whiskies (20 cents), but Paul didn't care to spend his money on drinks.

The landlady would accept $10 in certificates as part payment for the four weeks he still owed at his boarding house. Then Paul took off his shoes and pulled out two five dollar bills from under the lining. The landlady would have nothing to do with them. "Where did those come from?" she asked. Paul told her that his family in Denmark had given them to him when he left for America. The lady was a native of California and had never seen paper money. Those fives didn't look good to her. She called for Fred.

Fred was a pal with a good sense of humor. "Let's have some fun," he said to Paul. He told the landlady to call the police. She did, and when they came they took one look at Paul and asked her, "What has he been up to now?"

During the strike I had to get around to the different police stations to get permits for street meetings; these police officers knew me well; they always made fun of my accent and my bad English. The lady told them about the paper money-- they took a look at it, then gave her a credit slip for it and told her they would see her again.

I hope she got her money because the next day Fred and I left by train for Santa Barbara, where Fred told me we could get work at the big hotel.

The train pulled into the depot in Santa Barbara during the night; they waited there until dawn. Fred had been told that there was work available at the Hotel Potter. Landing a job was not difficult in this fast-growing seaside town, soon to be tagged the "America Riviera." It was indeed easy for Fred, who went right to the kitchen. As soon as he identified himself as a cook, there were no further questions asked -- he went to work at once.

Paul had to be more creative

I went in the front door and up to the desk where a clerk immediately gave me the register to sign. I had to tell him I was looking for a job. I don't believe he knew what I was talking about, but when he finally understood, he said, "Absolutely not. We don't need help." At that moment a gentleman with two suitcases came up to the desk, registered and was given the key to his room. He nodded to me, standing there in my white jacket and blue trousers. He assumed I was one of the hotel staff. I took the suitcases, went with him to the elevator, made sure everything in the room was in order. opened the window and asked if there was anything else he wanted. He gave me a twenty-five cent tip.

I went back to the lobby. "Now do you understand? That's the kind of job I'd like to have." I was hired as a bellhop and earned five dollars a week, and about five dollars a day in tips. Fred didn't make that much but he had some money and he didn't care.

We stayed at the Hotel Potter for two months before we decided to quit and go to Los Angeles.

> *The owner of the hotel liked both of us and asked us to stay on until he got some other help from Los Angeles or San Francisco. We stayed on two more weeks and when we left the owner gave us an extra week's pay and told us to come back any time.*

Los Angeles was a bad choice at the time; the city was full of men looking for work. Fred and Paul opted for a camping trip instead and got themselves outfitted for it They went west to Pasadena, where they rented a room together.

> *Pasadena, with its many different trees was the most fascinating town I had ever seen. We looked around for a few days, then set out for the nearby mountains. We went on foot to Mount Lowe, Mount Wilson and the Echo Mountains. There are different ways to get to the top of the mountains, but as we had plenty of time we walked and climbed. The mountains are not too high, some five to six thousand feet, and the hiking was very easy. The weather was beautiful and the view from the mountains down to the valley with its orange groves was just glorious*

> *We camped for about six weeks, then went back to Pasadena. Our room was ready for us, and the people who owned the house did not want rent for the time we had been away.*

> *Fred found some mail awaiting his arrival; one letter was from his two older brothers (24 and 26) They were about to take off on a camping trip, and asked if he wanted to go with them. Fred wrote back right away saying that we wanted to go and asking them to wait a few days.*

> *This meant a pleasant stop at Fred's family home in Riverside The city itself was beautiful, with a double row of pepper trees along Magnolia Avenue, which must have been ten miles long. We bought some new equipment and were ready to go a couple of days after we arrived.*

> *The trip up Mount San Antonio, also known as Old Baldy, and the hunting and fishing were something new for me. I just loved it, and my three fine friends were ready to help me along in every way. We were away for three weeks.*

> *Fred's two brothers had to get back to help with the oranges. We offered our help, but they didn't want us—had plenty of help, they said.*

"Now I want you to see Grand Canyon!" Fred was especially eager to show the place he knew so well to his friend Paul. It was important to get there before the weather set in. They boarded the train heading north from Los Angeles.

The manager of the hotel on the rim gave them a hearty welcome; he was especially glad to know that they had worked at the hotel in Santa Barbara, and asked them to stay on and work for two weeks. Most of his help had left after Labor Day, and he still had too many guests left to handle with the staff he had left.

> *We accepted the offer; in our spare time Fred took great pleasure in showing me the Grand Canyon—a wonderful experience. The sunsets and the early mornings when the sun started to come over the mountains were wonderful.*
>
> *In the evening after dinner there was a dance in the lobby; we were invited to take part. There were plenty of ladies, not too many men. Usually, we took as partners a group of girls from El Paso. Fred fell in love with one of them, and when it was time to leave he went with them to Texas. They wanted me to go along, but I refused. I was afraid that I too would fall in love. I just had a lot to see in the USA before I settled down.*
>
> *Fred wrote me later that he had been married, and his father-in-law had asked them to name something for their wedding present. They took him up on it and chose a large orange grove and a new house not far from Fred's family in California. They got it. Later Fred started a hotel in Riverside.*

Paul did not lose track of his good friend Fred. The two of them kept in touch. He was back in San Francisco when a letter came from Fred inviting him to come for an extended visit with him and his wife in their new home near Riverside. Paul was quick to accept the invitation. By the next week he was on his way south.

More Outdoor Adventures

The visit in Riverside was a good one; the young folks enjoyed each other's company and the many friends who often came for dinner and socializing. Paul was also a frequent guest in the home of Fred's parents, who lived nearby.

Fred's uncle was close at hand as well; he too had a large orange grove. Paul was a regular visitor there. One day Mr. Sanchez suggested that Paul join him and two other friends on a month's hunting trip in the area between the Grand Canyon and Colorado Springs, and Paul was happy to accept the offer.

To be quite certain that Paul had everything required for the trip, Mr. Sanchez supervised it all, from the rifle and fishing rod to the hiking boots. Paul was asked to pick out a rifle from his collection; he had a dozen of them, all polished and clean.

"Are you a good shot?" he asked, pointing to the picture of a deer painted on a board wall. "Aim for the heart." Paul did and hit the heart 11 times out of 12. "Couldn't do that good!" said Mr. Sanchez.

Finally he was satisfied with all the preparations. "Everything seems to be okay," he said. "Let's go! He was in charge of all the transportation costs and arrangements for the four of them.

The first lap of the trip was to have been by train to Flagstaff and Grand Canyon. The others would have liked to go farther south, but Paul was not enthusiastic about the heat, so they agreed to continue northward. By train, stagecoach and horseback they headed toward Colorado Springs and the area known today as Rocky Mountain National Park..

Once there, they had before them "America's Mountain" – Pikes Peak, as well as Long's Peak and their glorious natural surroundings. There was a cog railway, and a carriage road to the summit of Pike's Peak. An automobile had gone up there in 1901. But the men walked; like Paul they loved the great views and the sounds and sights of nature.

Not until Mr. Sanchez had shown me everything worth seeing at Colorado Springs did we go camping and hunting. It was just marvelous all the way. We never shot or fished any more than we could eat. The mountains were beautiful, the water was clear and the air so refreshing. We had no tent or sleeping bags, just our blankets. And we marveled as the endless black night opened above us, lit only by the stars.

Snakes would bother us at times Once I asked Jim, one of the other men in our party, "Say, Jim, what kind of snake is this?" I had picked one up by the neck and he made a lot of noise. "Rattler," said Jim. "Throw it away. He is poisonous." It didn't take me long to get rid of the beast, which was only about three feet long.

Mr. Sanchez still had plans left over for Grand Canyon. The group went back there, to find surprisingly few people around. Perhaps, Paul thought, it was the wrong time of year, or perhaps the price for rooms at the hotel was too high -- $ 3 per night!

Mr. Sanchez told us we were going to the bottom of the canyon the next morning. At 5A.M. we got underway; we could have rented horses, but preferred to walk the five miles down. It was quite a walk, but also a most wonderful one.. I had never seen anything so gorgeous; I wondered if a painter could get all the colors on canvas. From above, the Colorado River had looked like a small stream Coming closer we could see what a mighty giant it was. I wouldn't have wanted to travel on it in a boat or canoe. We spent five days at the river, then went back up to the rim, tired but otherwise feeling fine.

From the Grand Canyon we went back to Colorado Springs, on foot or by train or stagecoach. We saw one wonderful scene after another; we couldn't get enough of beautiful Colorado.. Mountain trout and wild game were plentiful; we ate a lot of both. For me it was paradise.

One day in the mountains they came across a cabin with a sign on the door "Walk in, but close the door!" Inside they found enough food and dry wood to last the four of them for a week. They enjoyed the rest there, and before they left they supplied the cabin with food for the next four people who would come along. They bought the food at a store some ten miles away. The cabin was owned by a doctor from San Diego. His name and address were in a book on the table, in which guests were asked to sign their names. They did this, and also cut enough firewood to last a winter.

The men continued north as far as the city of Aspen, then back to Colorado Springs and from there to Denver, where they parted It was back to Riverside for Mr. Sanchez and his two friends. And Paul returned to San Francisco.

Good place for hiking

Good job to try

The Greatest Adventure

An Exciting New Prospect

Paul's brother was back at work as a contractor – the two of them went their own ways. There were plenty of hamburger stands in San Francisco. Paul found a good job in one of them at 22nd and Mission Street. It was nice to become reacquainted with the Danes and enjoy good times with them.

In 1911, though, he decided to go back to Los Angeles. Working for wages in America did not really appeal to him, and he still cherished the dream of going into business for himself.

One morning walking along Spring Street I ran across a man selling hot dogs on the street. I bought one, then asked him the old question: "How's business?" "No good," he said. "Want to sell out?" "Sure. How much will you pay me?" Twenty five dollars." He was willing to sell. He told me where to get the frankfurters and the rolls, then turned over his machine, a square metal box with a container for hot water with the hot dogs, and a charcoal fire and warming compartment for the rolls. He got the $25. I got the business

"Hot dogs – red hot – ten cents!" was my call. By 10 o'clock I had always sold them all – five cents profit on each. 100 hot dogs –$10. $5 profit. Not bad.

At 11 P.M. I went to a night club in Pasadena, where I had a job seating the guests. "Captain" I was called. I made $5 at that place every night. Things were looking up. I usually quit about 4 or 5 in the morning. Then I usually went to a church – any church. In those days a church was a good place to go to in the early morning. You could sit and rest and meditate. Nobody bothered you. If you had money you *just dropped it in the box. I had had a good day and a better night and thought I would share it with the pope. I dropped a couple of five dollar gold pieces in a glass container in the Catholic church I had entered and then sat down, talking to myself..*

The gentleman who had entered right behind me also sat down, just a few pews behind me. I stayed an hour. So did he. Leaving the church, he spoke to me.

> *"I'd like to talk with you. Do you know me?"*

> *"Yes, in a way.. You sometimes come to the club where I have a part-time job. And if I remember right you also bought a hot dog from me last night."*

> *(Laughing) "What else?"*

> *"That's all."*

> *"Good. I am also interested in two hotels here, and in the summer time I go to Yellowstone Park. I am the superintendent there. Now I like you. Would you like to work with me?"*

> *"In a hotel, no."*

> *"Well, in the last part of May I go to Yellowstone. Would you like to go there?"*

> *"Absolutely. When do we go?"*

That made the man laugh. He gave Paul his card

> *"I'll see you again Come and see me at this address on the first of May."*

Paul went home to his room and his bed, thinking to himself that he might be traveling again pretty soon.

It was only about a week later that Mr. Farrow came to the night club and asked Paul to see him the next day at the Hotel Raymond in Pasadena. There he was told about the job in

Yellowstone Park. He was also asked to quit his job and come to work for Mr. Farrow the following day. Paul would be working for him in the office and during the season go to the park as steward. He was also introduced to Mr. Adler, the chef at the Hotel Raymond. He too would be going to Yellowstone.. In the few months before they left he saw a great deal of Mr. Adler and was often invited to visit in his home in Pasadena.

Paul was also introduced, always as "Mr. Hansen", in the customary manner of the day, to half a dozen clerks working in Mr. Farrow's office. There were no girls in the office.

In front of these clerks, Mr. Farrow told Paul that "These people would all like to go to Yellowstone, but they are all married and their wives won't let them go." Was he just kidding.? Paul was not sure. In any case, he got on with the work, was shown the bookkeeping system used in Yellowstone, and many other office procedures.

Otherwise Mr. Farrow used him more as an office boy and messenger than anything else. Often he took him along for lunch. One day he asked about Paul's winter clothes. "Don't have any," was the response. "All right, we'll get you some and charge it to your account." Mr. Farrow paid for it all, but refused to take Paul's money when he tried to pay for the clothes at the end of the season.

When business demands called him to Fargo, North Dakota in mid-May, Mr. Farrow's valued helper was "Mr. Hansen." At 5 A.M. on the morning after their arrival in Fargo, he found his boss at the door of his hotel room. He had to go to another town by stagecoach, and was leaving important work in Paul's hands. He gave him a list of ten persons to be interviewed for jobs in Yellowstone Under no circumstances was anyone to be promised a job whose name was not on the list. With this accomplished he was to go by train to Bismark, where they would meet at the Northwest Hotel.

There was time for a last snooze before Paul appeared in the hotel lobby, at 8 A.M. asking to have a room set up for the interviewing.. With his breakfast he was given an envelope with last minute instructions and $200 to cover expenses.

> *I noticed that no interviews were scheduled before 10 A.M. I had the time for a walk around the town. The weather was cold and there was snow on the ground, however I was well prepared and didn't mind the cold.*

At 10 o'clock I was back at the Waldorf, where we had stayed overnight. It was a fine hotel and the manager asked me if there was anything he could do for me.; he would be happy to help. He noticed my lack of English and, of course, had to find out where I came from. It turned out that his parents had come to the U.S.A. from Denmark, and he spoke the language very well. I told him that about all I needed was for someone to take care of the people who would show up during the day and to not let more than two people in at one time.

My list had only ten people; they all came during the morning hours and by 1 o'clock I was finished and ready to have lunch and take off for Bismark. As it happened, I stayed in Fargo another night; it was too late to get a train that day, but the next day I set out for the capital.

I enjoyed the train ride through the country; those prairie farms are really enormously large. A man sitting next to me told me that sometimes there would be two dozen plows at work at one time on a farm.. What else he told me I am afraid went over my head; his American language was too much for me, and he spoke very fast and did not expect any answers.

At Bismark I went to the Northwest Hotel, where I was to meet Mr. Farrow. He did not arrive for several days, which gave me a chance to see the town, the capitol building and the Missouri River, which is very wide there.

When Mr. Farrow finally arrived he had much to tell, but was also very busy for a few days. Then we had to go to Livingstone, Montana and to Gardiner.

That was all for now; the snow was too deep in Yellowstone. Back we went to Los Angeles.

Yellowstone 1911

Paul's meeting with Mr. Farrow was the beginning of a meaningful relationship. The perceptive older man, experienced and respected in the business world, had been quick to recognize the value of the bright young fellow he had observed in several very different settings. He knew a good man when he met one. If youth was a factor, it was here only an asset, Could the young man make adequate use of the English language? – So far so good, and certainly his ability to learn was unimpaired

For Paul, the relationship with his new friend opened doors to new worlds of knowledge and experience. The months of waiting to set foot at Yellowstone were filled for him with constant new learning and activity, all of it related to the wonderful new experience that awaited him.

Yellowstone! Since its establishment as the first national park in the United States – the first such park anywhere in the world – the name brought a thrill of excitement to those who spoke it. If, like Paul, they contemplated actually experiencing its wonders, they counted the days until their actual arrival there.. Pinpointing that precise day could be challenging. Hard winters in northwest Wyoming, where the major part of the vast park is located, could necessitate prolonged snow removal before general admittance to the workers and the public was granted. This was also the case in 1911. Departure for the Park was delayed by heavy snowstorms until the end of May. Not until then could Paul join the other workers and board the special train headed north from Los Angeles to Yellowstone National Park..

By then there were about a hundred persons waiting to board the special train. It had sleepers, dining car and whatever else went with the special. The train went to the west entrance of Yellowstone, where we got in stagecoaches and started out for the various hotels and lunch stations to get them ready for the opening on the 15th of June. Quite a number of the employees went with Mr. Farrow to Mammoth Hot Springs, the headquarters of the Yellowstone Park Association, which had charge of the hotels.

I went with Mr. Adler to the Lake Hotel at Norris Hot Springs. It was bitterly cold when we arrived, but the winter-keeper and his wife had some long tables set up in the kitchen, which was warm and cozy. There were about forty of us in all. We had

a big plate of vegetable soup, steak large and plentiful, potatoes and vegetables, coffee and apple pie. It all sure tasted good on that cold day.

After our good meal at Norris Hot Springs, we left and started out slow but sure, towards the Canon Hotel. It was snowing all the way and now and then we had to get out and shovel away drifts. Eventually we got there and another great meal was prepared for us and served immediately, as they had anticipated the hour of our arrival.

The next morning after breakfast, about a dozen of us went back to the Lake Hotel. As we left the Canon the snow was still coming down and the return to the Lake Hotel was slow. When we got there we had to enter by the rear as the snow was too deep at the front doors. After a good lunch we were taken to our rooms. I had a cottage for myself, but the rest all had rooms in the main building. During the day everyone pitched in and we soon had the front cleared of all snow and got started on the various other tasks getting the hotel ready for the opening on June 15

In that summer of 1911. increasing numbers of eager tourists found their way to the "wonderland" that was repeatedly termed "the best idea America ever had." It was now about 40 years since that special region of the backwaters of the Yellowstone River was thus distinguished. By an act of congress in 1872 Yellowstone became the world's first national park, "reserved and withdrawn from settlement, occupancy or sale." and set apart for the benefit and enjoyment of the people."

The people wanted not only pleasure but information. They wanted to know and understand the natural processes that created the geysers and other geothermal wonders that fascinated and delighted them. Rangers and other well-informed persons were hired or volunteered to give talks or conduct walking tours throughout the park, which comprised over two million acres, almost three times the size of Switzerland.

Paul was fortunate to meet with some of those who were glad to share their special knowledge.

There were two gentlemen from New York that I liked very much. One was interested in geology, the other in biology. I met them in the Teton Mountains one time I went there for a short camping trip by myself. They came very often to the Old Faithful Inn. Sometimes I would go there with Mr. Farrow and the four of us had a real good time together. They loved to talk about rocks and plants, It was interesting to listen to them discussing the different things.

In 1911 many people did their park touring by stagecoach, which was handled by the Yellowstone Park Transportation Company. They had excellent stagecoaches, seating from three to eight people. All of the hotels were served. The trip from Mammoth Hot Springs, Livingstone or Gardiner took about six days and cost $50 including all meals and rooms. Another way to go, with departure from Gardiner, was with the Wylie Permanent Camp Company. They had camps several places in the Park and fine tents. The sleeping quarters were good and comfortable and their transportation was good too. The cost for the trip around the Park, including all meals and sleeping facilities was $35.

As an employee that summer, Paul's work was mostly at the Lake Hotel, but often also at the Canon. The 18 mile trip between the two hotels was sometimes unexpectedly harrowing.

Once I even drove a four-horse team from the Canon to the Lake. I had gone to the Canon in the afternoon and found that the meat truck was to leave the next morning early for the Lake. I asked for permission to go along with the truck and the driver said it was okay with him. It turned out to be a hectic trip.

Some places the road goes along the Yellowstone River and there are many interesting places to view like the "mud cauldron," which I think is one of the weirdest sights in the Park. It is a circular crater some 35 feet deep. The bottom is full of boiling mud, rising in pasty bubblings. Now and then there are violent eruptions. It could be the devil himself, I thought, who has his residence down below, and some of his guests are trying to escape through the mud crater.

A couple of miles out from the Canon we noticed a number of bears in the middle of the road and our young horses got panicky. Quickly I turned the reins over to the driver. (I was driving the wagon with the four rather wild horses at the time.) Good thing that I did because even the old, experienced driver had a hard time getting by the bears.

That particular morning I think we met bears half a dozen times, but after the first encounter I managed real well and drove all the way to the Lake. Even got a compliment from the driver. "In a few years," said he, "you will be good enough to take over a stagecoach with six people in it."

In August the steward of the Lake Hotel took sick and was unable to work. Paul took his place and liked the hotel and the surroundings so much that he asked to go back there again the following season.

He always met people that he liked in the hotels and camping grounds. One man and his wife that he met during the last month of the Yellowstone season invited him to stay with them on their farm in Idaho after the season ended. They promised to meet him in Mammoth on the 16th of September, after the Park closed. They asked him to stay with them until Yellowstone reopened in 1912. They thought maybe he was coming back, and of course they were right. Paul asked them about hunting and fishing. "Plenty," they said. "Our daughter will be happy to take you, but watch out – she is something of a wildcat –20 years old and she loves animals, horses especially!"

On the 15th of September the season closed and Paul went to the Mammoth to meet the Conleys. They were there, and on the 17th he set off with them on his winter vacation. About Yellowstone he later wrote:

> *Yellowstone is a wonder and in the two seasons I was there I saw pretty much all of it, from Mammoth Hot Springs to the Fountain Hotel, Old Faithful, Thumb Lunch Station and West Yellowstone Station.––Everything near and around those sites I accessed on foot, on horseback or by stagecoach. I also went to Jackson and the Tetons. Going with Mr. Farrow meant a lot to me. I marveled at everything I saw..*

YELLOWSTONE 1911-12

Lake Hotel

Making friends with a very young bear

Meat truck from the ranch

Groceries from Gardiner, Montana

A day's catch from the lake

Bears......

Winter Vacation in Idaho – Indian Prophecies

The Conley party headed south, past Jackson Hole and the Teton Mountains, then south-westward into Idaho. The journey was made in part by train or stagecoach, and nearing ranch country, by the Conley carriage, sent out to meet them on the way. All told it took about a week.

The Conley ranch was very large, with at least a dozen men in charge of the thousands of cattle. There was a fine house. The first one to rush out from it to meet them was Grace, the daughter, who had been accurately described by her parents: an outdoor girl, full of life and fun. wild as a young horse. Paul thought he had learned all about wild horses at Yellowstone, but she could outride anyone on the ranch, including her father and mother, who were experts. Her brother, at 18, had just started college. That was of no interest to Grace, who loved animals, riding, hunting and fishing.

Mealtimes at the ranch were something to watch: there were ten hands and we all sat at the same table in the large kitchen for our meals. Mr. Conley would say grace beginning, "Father in Heaven – keep your fingers off those biscuits, Jim, -- we thank you, -- Gene, there are three chops for each of you, --for what -- that jam you can leave alone, Arthur. -- for what we are about to receive – put that butter back, and right now, Charlie,-- and it better be good. Amen." Everything was good, and it would all be on the table, including water, milk and coffee.

The cook also ate at the table with the rest of us. He was an Indian, but I never did find out exactly where he really came from.. He took care of everything and never asked for help. Mrs. Conley gave him the menu, that's all. He was a splendid cook. Sometimes I used to help him in the kitchen, as did Mrs Conley, and the daughter.

Eski (or Onez) and I became good friends. He taught me his language, and I tried to teach him Danish, but he would have nothing to do with "that stuff", he said -- "Indian language much better."

One of Eski's hobbies was carving totem poles; he used only his pocket knife -- hard work for him. I asked him to make me one. He said he would, but it would take a long time.. I said never mind, I wouldn't know where to tell him to send it anyway. He said he would make it, but I wouldn't get it until after I came back from the war This was news to me; I didn't know of any war. He told me that I would go to fight in a big war; I would go over a very big pond – many days to cross. I would fight but I would not get killed. When I got back from the war I would find the totem pole in my room. And, he told me, I should not look for my squaw here; I would find her later across the big water. And I would become a very old man – maybe sixty!

Who was Eski? From which of the multiple native American tribes did he come? What was the Indian tongue that Paul Hansen from Denmark learned to speak? What was the nature of their customs, the crafts they would seem to have shared generously and openly with their foreign visitor, the songs and dances he observed or in which he took part? None of this was recorded for us to read today. It was simply experienced and enjoyed by one who viewed his Indian acquaintances as he would any other friendly neighbors.

Strange and surprising predictions Paul heard from his Indian friend! Would it all come true? Time would tell. In due course this story of his life in America will also tell. But now it is time to reveal more about Idaho and Paul's memorable winter vacation there well over a hundred years ago.

There were many Indians in our neighborhood in Idaho in 1911. I very often went to their dances and parties and got to know their customs and language pretty well. I got so many of their handmade trinkets, blankets and heaven knows what that I put it all in a trunk I had in my room. Some day maybe I can sell it, I thought.

Grace and I often went riding. All the horses were young and wild. We both took our rifles along and if we saw game we thought worthwhile we would hunt and kill. Grace didn't care much for fishing, but I went once in a while. There were lots of trout in the streams and they were very easy to catch as no one else was around to bother you.

The fall arrived and the winter was severe, with lots of snow, but it was a good life on the ranch. Twice during the winter I went with Mr. and Mrs. Conley and Grace to visit their relatives in Pocatello. These were pleasant trips which we all enjoyed very much.

The Conleys would have liked Grace and me to fall in love and get married, but I was not cut out for farm life and early marriage. I had a lot to see of the United States and preferred single life for some years yet. Grace didn't care. The family had plenty of money and she had lots of friends in Pocatello.

Yellowstone 1912

Spring came, and with it a letter for Paul, from Mr. Farrow, in which was included an application form for the 1912 Yellowstone Season. Was he ready to sign up again? There was no doubt about that! Paul returned the form and sent a separate letter to Mr. Farrow to find out what he wanted him to do. In his return letter Mr. Farrow asked him to please come to Los Angeles at once where his help was needed.

He left Idaho with the warm wishes of good people, the new friends who had given him a memorable winter vacation.

In Los Angeles it was good to be needed and wanted. Most of the required work was familiar to Paul after the previous year's orientation. By the 15th of May they were ready to prepare the crew to leave on the special train for Yellowstone. This time Paul left someone else in charge, and went north with Mr. Farrow to places where business matters required his attention.. They went to Bismark and Fargo in North Dakota, then south to Mammoth and Livingstone in Montana. It was opening day in Yellowstone before they made it back there on June 15.

Paul went to the Lake Hotel, where he stayed as steward all through the season. Most of the employees were new; there was a new manager too, and a new chef, again a very good one. There were good relations all around, and as Paul put it himself, "I just got to love that place."

Two of his associates whom Paul described as "fine men" became his good friends. The transportation agent at the Lake, Mr. Johnson, was one of them, as was the manager of the boat company, Mr. Holland. The latter, who had come from the Thumb Lunch Station. also operated a store that sold all kinds of small articles to campers and tourists.

> *I had several chances to go camping in the mountains, never more than two days at a time. We had a fisherman at the hotel; he caught for the different hotels in the park on an average of 200 pounds of trout per day, and was paid fifteen cents per pound. I went with him whenever I had time. He was a good fisherman who knew how to throw a line. It was a tiresome job, though – too easy to get the fish! They would bite on anything moving.*

Shooting was not allowed, so no game was ever served the guests while I was there.

There was lots of time to see all of Yellowstone and going with Mr. Farrow meant a lot to me.

Before I went to the Park I had been told that the bears were very friendly and almost tame. Not quite so! Once on a walk, only a few miles from Old Faithful Inn, a guest and I encountered a large grizzly bear who showed no friendly intentions whatsoever. He started to chase me; I fell over an old tree on the ground with the bear right on top of me. He sure enough didn't kill me, but the doctor at Livingstone put me in the hospital for a week while he repaired my wounds and bruises.

Another time a man came running up to my cottage at the Lake Hotel about 9 P.M. with his arm torn off by a bear. He and his family were camping down at the lake when a few bears came and molested them. The man started to hit one of the bears with a baseball bat. I guess the bear got annoyed and took both bat and arm from the poor fellow. It was too late for the man; he died a few days later. We didn't have a doctor at the hotel at the time.

Sometimes a couple of wagonloads of groceries would arrive at the hotel at the same time.. They usually had eight mules or horses to draw the wagons, and with the help of all the men and boys at the hotel I would manage to unload the wagons in no time.. I took pictures of the proceedings and promised a copy to everyone who would help. That usually was effective. Sometimes as we unloaded, a couple of bears would climb up on the load to sniff around, mostly for sugar. I always warned the guests not to feed the bears sugar. The bears would be watching as they took it from their pockets. Then it was no more sugar – the coat would be torn from the man and carried into the woods, with the bear still looking for sugar from the coat. Or, as I had seen, the fellow might have his arm torn off by the bear.

Once the park season got really going, a lot of garbage would be left for the bears about a mile from the hotels. That gave the guests a good look and good pictures of the bears. They didn't care for people when there was garbage to be had..

I understand there is better control of the bears nowadays. Yet I would still say <u>don't trust them!</u>

At the time I was there the Park was first under the control of the Secretary of the Interior. Later U.S. cavalry under the war department were stationed at different points in the Park. There was a post about two miles from the Lake Hotel. They were all young fellows and I often went there for information, a chat and a game of poker. The cavalry men got fifteen dollars a month salary so I can't say our games were costly for any of us.

I was one of the few people allowed out in the woods after 10 P.M., and when I went home around 12 or 1 A.M. a couple of the boys always saddled their horses and rode along. It was mostly grizzlies we would meet on the road, and of course they were no match for three fellows on horseback. Up the hill they would beat us, but going down they almost fell over themselves if they ran too fast.

Only once did I ride home alone and of course that was the time I got lost in the dark. I thought I would take a shortcut and that led to my downfall. The watchman at the hotel asked the cavalry post about 3 A.M. why I hadn't gone home, and when the cavalry men answered that I had left at 11 o'clock, they sent half a dozen boys out to look for me. I had got tired riding around, had started a fire, and that's where they found me about 4 A.M., sound asleep, not far from my house.. No harm done, only the boys didn't like the job of riding around in the dark of the night.. I never went home alone after that.

Toward the end of the 1912 season I was also able to go back to the Tetons and Jackson Hole south of the park to meet my two friends of the year before.. We were well equipped for a trip and enjoyed it immensely What beautiful scenery, and the fresh air and water! I sure did hope it would remain that way for many years.

Often in those two summers roaming the mountains and valleys I would be thinking what a wonderful country we have -- the marvelous animal life, with no hunting allowed., the birds, the bears, the buffaloes that were actually without interest in a couple of young fellows walking alone through the woods. And then the pure air and clear water with mountain trout we could practically take right out of the water when we went for a swim

The time came for closing the Park for the season. On the 15th of September the last guest had left. The cleanup began and at 2 P.M. the stagecoaches were ready to leave, some for Mammoth, some for West Yellowstone Station. That evening only the winter-keeper, his wife and I occupied the hotel.

How I had come to love that Park, the mountains, the lake, the rivers, the people! After that second season I never did see Mr. Farrow, or Yellowstone again.

Special Trip to Washington State

Paul's good friends, the Conleys, were not yet ready to say goodbye. They had invited Paul to join them on a trip westward to Washington State. On the morning of September 15th two surreys drew up to the front door of the Lake Hotel. The extra surrey had been engaged, with two boys in charge,, to transport the purchases made in Livingstone back to the ranch.

For Mrs Conley this was principally a shopping trip. She was a lady of refined tastes and discrimination who knew where to find the products she wanted to satisfy her desires for her own personal use and for the personalized environment she created in house and home. Livingstone was a good shopping center and both surreys were sent home from there well loaded with the Conley purchases. The travelers went on by railroad to Butte, another thriving city in Montana, where Mr. Conley had many friends.

They were not satisfied until Paul had viewed the copper and silver mines there, which he found highly interesting. Three days were spent in Butte, always, as everywhere, in fine hotels at 4 dollars per night.

From Butte the travelers went on to Spokane, in Washington State, located in the center of agriculture. The city had two waterfalls that furnished water power for many, many factories, for the electric cars and for electric lights in the city. Spokane also had a fine opera house – of particular interest to Paul, the opera fan. A couple of days were spent in Spokane before they set off for Tacoma, close to Mt Rainier, where Grace joined them.

Tacoma was then about 35 years old. Already it had a number of fine buildings: opera house, Carnegie Library, the City Hall and others. There were good roads from Tacoma to a place called Natural Parks, a beautiful place carpeted with flowers and lots of trees and lakes.

I was very anxious to get to Mount Rainier, or Mount Tacoma, as it was also called. Grace also wanted to climb with her father and me, but Mrs. Conley did not want to go along. She would do some shopping in Tacoma while we were gone. We had camping equipment with us and wanted to see if we could get to the top of the mountain, about 14,500 feet.

We set off for Wilkerson by train. From Wilkerson there was a good bridle path to a place some 7-8000 feet above the sea. From this point there was a good view onto some of the glaciers on the mountain, but climbing to the summit from this particular point was too much for me. Mr. Conley did not want to try it either. So down we went, to the great disgust of Grace, who would have liked to get to the top. We went around to the south side of Mount Rainier, to "Paradise Park" We had a good time, some fine walks, and climbing, but we never got to the summit. I believe we could have made it from where we were, but time was running out. .We had been away a week, and Mr. Conley wanted to get back to his wife in Tacoma

She was happy to see us back with no broken bones and in good shape She had never liked the idea of Grace's going along; she knew her daughter and knew she was always willing to take chances.

From Tacoma we went directly to Portland. For me the city and the surroundings were very interesting. The Conleys had to promise to take me sightseeing some other time as they had been called back and left for home the following day.

I went on from Portland to Seattle and Vancouver and by steamboat to Victoria and Vancouver Island. Being alone I was very quickly tired of walking around. I went back to Seattle and got a boat from there to San Francisco.

Life in San Francisco 1912-1916

San Francisco was still the active, lively city with which Paul had become familiar. When he returned there in the fall of 1912 there were family surprises awaiting him. While he was away his brother Walter had been married: Margit was a vivacious new sister-in-law. His sister Ellen had married and come from Denmark. Another sister, Agnes, had also immigrated and was in New York City. She and her new husband were expected to settle eventually in California.

Once more Paul had no trouble finding a good job in one of the many small "hamburger stands", often owned by Danes or by people whose parents had come from Denmark.. He enjoyed the work, made good wages and was glad to be re-acquainted with Danish friends and to join in the lively social activities of the Danish clubs. There were many Scandinavians all over California; they were well liked and were successful in business or in their own individual efforts of various kinds.

Paul joined the YMCA and loved the association with new friends who shared his age and interests.

> *It was a wonderful organization to belong to. Many of the boys were of my age, and not only did we have a good time, but I was able to keep fit in health and spirit. We often went on long excursions, always camping. Of all the places we visited I liked Yosemite Valley the best. Of course I hadn't been around to some of the famous places as yet, but at that time I thought there couldn't be anything in the world compared to Yosemite Valley.*

> *I believe one of our favorite camping trips was to the Santa Cruz Mountains, Monterey and the beach at Santa Cruz.*

Another and nearer place for a day's outing was to Mount Tamalpais. We used to take the ferry to Sausalito, then go by electric train to Mill Valley. From there we would hike along a fine trail to the top of Mount Tamalpais There was a winding railway running up to the top also, but I don't remember ever using it.

I very seldom worked on Sunday. The family usually got together at someone's house or we took our meal along to Golden Gate Park or to the beach. We had a good Danish church, but Danish or American I went to church every Sunday. Sometimes, of course, we boys from the YMCA had decided to go camping, and even at that, someone in the bunch would give a short talk and we would sing a few hymns

In 1915 the great "Panama Pacific International Exposition" came to San Francisco, a singular distinction less than 10 years after the disastrous earthquake that had almost wiped out the city in 1906. The basic preparations alone for this World's Fair required months of time and effort. Space had to be created by filling in 630 acres of marshland. On this new land 47 miles of walkways were built and 31 nations from all over the world, as well as from some of the United States, created exhibition halls and demonstrations.

Like every other resident, Paul had a ticket to "the Fair" as it was always called. It was good for any day, all day....for all of the many days until the end of November, when it would all come to an end. Paul was fascinated by the many technological glimpses of the future, the many things that we take for granted today, automobiles and airplanes, telephones and movies. Henry Ford, who had made automobiles financially available for many Americans, actually built an assembly line at the fair where Model T Fords were produced three hours a day, six days a week.

During these years in San Francisco, Paul also became an American citizen. He loved to tell of how, after the formalities, the judge engaged in a private conversation with him. "I see that you're from Denmark," said the judge. "Have you read Hamlet?" "Of course," Paul replied. "He was a Dane, you know, and his castle is in Denmark. Naturally I have been there." -- 'Well, that's good enough for me." said the judge, as he put the official stamp on the citizenship document.

Paul had kept in touch with his friends, the Conleys. Some time after returning from his trip to Washington State with them he had heard that the reason for their cutting short the trip so suddenly was that a telegram had informed them that their house on the ranch had caught fire and was a total loss. Though many things had been saved, thanks to the quick action of the men who left the breakfast table in a hurry, they were unable to access the attic, where Paul's belongings were stored. It was not a great loss: mostly winter clothing. A trunk full of Indian artifacts given him by his Indian friends was lost, With it, the unresolved questions concerning the life and culture of his Indian friends, especially about the totem pole, might have been answered

Paul was told that a new and better house was being built, with a special room for him if he were to come again.

Now in January, 1916 they sent me a first class round trip ticket and an invitation to their daughter's wedding, to be held in Pocatello. It was real nice of them and I accepted –went there the 15th of January. Of course I had to get something for my good friend Grace. The one and only thing she was interested in was horses, and I was lucky. Over in Oakland I found just the right thing. –a fine looking bronze horse about a foot high and weighing 70 pounds. It put me back $120, but it was worth it. Never have I seen anyone that happy over a gift. Her parents also liked it. Mr. Conley gave me a slap on the back that sent me rolling along the floor. What a man – six feet two and in the best of health!

The party after the wedding ceremonies was given at the Pacific Hotel – a very large party, and of course everything to eat that could be made available with money. Mr. Conley wasn't surprised, but most of the men could not understand that I did not get drunk. For every toast given I emptied my quite large glass. When, towards the finish, I made a speech, I don't believe a man at the table was sober or understood a word of what I was saying. But Grace and her mother did, I knew they were because they were laughing and were happy, as I was. They emptied their glasses and then smashed them after the talk. It was a good party with fine people. Grace got a good husband, a good ranch-man, a jolly one.

Panama Pacific International Exposition

San Francisco 1915

Tower of Jewels

Denmark Building

43

Coast to Coast in a Model-T Ford

Paul's brother Walter was mechanically inclined; he followed with interest the activities of other young men working on their own to produce a horseless buggy. In Michigan a self-taught engineer, Henry Ford, engaged a group of able contemporaries to approach the project with organized, practical methods.. A series of model cars was developed at the Ford Motor Company; among them the Model T, known popularly as The Tin Lizzie, emerged as outstanding. It was the common man's affordable answer to the need for daily transportation: cheap, easy to maintain and operate, also on rough roads. In San Francisco, many were introduced to the Model T at the World's Fair in 1915.

Walter and his wife had asked me if I would like to go with them by automobile to New York. Of course I wanted very much to go. I was working in a café as a waiter and tried to make as much money as possible before setting out on the great adventure: the cross-continental tour California to New York in a Model T Ford.

We planned to start about the first of May, fully equipped for camping all the way. Walter figured it would take us six weeks.

The front seat of the car had been equipped with hinges, so that it could swing down and make a good bed for two. Tied on the side of the car was a fine tent with a waterproof floor. That was where I slept. We had a good gun and a fine fishing rod so we could hunt and fish wherever possible. There would be plenty of dry wood all the way; we expected no problem on that score. We took along a winch to pull us out of washouts in the event we got stuck somewhere in the desert, meaning we didn't exactly trust the Lincoln Highway all the way.

I wasn't used to the automobile as yet; a couple of good horses would have suited me better, only it would have taken a while longer to get to New York City.

His personal experiences with horses in the west and their trusted, and indispensable association with stagecoaches were known and familiar to Paul, as were the interstate railway connections. Roads were built for local needs or as they became necessary to cities not yet served by railways. The advent of automobiles and especially the World's Fair of 1915 in San Francisco, spurred the development of extended roads, that became known as highways. Though endorsed and promoted by such prominent and influential men as President Theodore Roosevelt and Thomas Edison and named in honor of Lincoln well before the dedication of the special monument in his honor in Washington, the new highway was mostly a dubious trail – a highway in name only.

But if the name of the road was a bit grand for what Paul described as "good for a horse and buggy, or for stagecoaches, but not for auto-mobiles," the spirits of the travelers were high as they set forth on the Lincoln Highway on the first day of May, 1916 in their Model T Ford.

> *We went to the ferry which took us to Oakland; from there it was fairly easy going to Sacramento and up to Lake Tahoe, where we spent a couple of days. Across Nevada it was tough going. The roads were bad and a few times we had trouble with the car and got stuck in washouts, but with the help of the winch we got out again and rolled on to Salt Lake City. We tried to follow the Lincoln Highway, but it was not always easy.*

> *We were lucky in meeting fine people all the way. If we were near a farm or some populated area, somebody would come out with a team of horses and pull us out if we were stuck. Not once did they accept our offered pay for their work. Instead they would ask us to stay overnight and get cleaned up and receive good meals. We were thankful for this.*

> *Down in Utah, not far from Grand Junction, Colorado, we went to a farm to get some eggs and butter and bread. The folks there were so interested in our model T that they asked us to stay for a few days. When we left after three days the man went along to Grand Junction and bought himself a car. Walter taught him how to drive it in one day.*

Daily life on their unchartered ways across the continent gradually made both men experts in the working operations of their Tin Lizzie. Paul too developed a new vocabulary. He was soon speaking of transmission bands, pistons and ignition coils. He knew how to start the car with the key instead of the crank, and when the key worked for him, he could often predict whether the car might take off forwards or backwards. He knew how to counter the effect of gravity when the gas level was low by backing up the steepest hills. If any one wanted a driving lesson he was happy to oblige. He had mastered the basics and could do it well

The drive across Colorado was just marvelous – beautiful rivers, good fishing and hunting, and the finest people you could ever think of meeting. Of course, I recognized a number of the places I had seen a few years before. The state, with its high mountains, is so wonderful to see that I wouldn't have minded staying there much longer than we did. We never had trouble finding a good place to camp overnight.

From Grand Junction we went to Glenwood Springs, then down to Aspen and to Colorado Springs. There are so many places to go to near this town that it was no wonder my brother had told us it would take six weeks for the trip to New York City. I believe we took in almost everything mentioned in our guide book and put a lot of mileage on our Tin Lizzie, but she held up real well.

Denver was the last city stop in Colorado. From there they headed toward Chicago. Nebraska, Iowa and Illinois were mostly farmland, with driving that was easy on the car and pleasant for the passengers. They enjoyed visits in Omaha and Davenport with old friends, or impromptu stops to camp and get acquainted with friendly strangers.

When we got to a place where we would like to camp, if it was near a farmhouse we would ask the owner if it was all right to camp at that particular spot. Very often we would be invited in for dinner and to stay overnight in their guest rooms. The people we met were always nice to us. In the evening we would sit in their living room at the open fireplace and talk about our trip and about life on the farm. A few times on Saturday nights we got an invitation to go to a dance with them in the nearest town.

On one large farm the owner and his wife were both from Norway. As Margit, Walter's wife, was also from Norway, they had a good time together talking about the old country. It happened to be a Friday afternoon we had driven up to their place, and they insisted on our staying until Monday, which we did. On Saturday we all went to a dance. It was a pleasure to see Margit having such a good time. She was lively and full of fun; the young people really enjoyed her company.

In this part of the country too, if we tried to buy eggs or butter or bread from farms, not once could we get anybody to accept payment. "That's all right," the man would say. Some day we will come to California; we'll look you up then." We always gave them our last address in California.

It was late evening when they arrived in Chicago. They had lost their way in the dark and were not quite sure how far they had come and where they were. They saw a river, trees and what looked like a nice place to camp. They halted, and as it was late, just had a sandwich and some milk for supper. Margit and Walter went to sleep in the car as usual and Paul put up his tent. He woke up at daylight; someone was talking to Walter. It proved to be a Chicago policeman who was telling his brother that they were in a city park. He thought it would be a good idea if they got underway since no parking or camping was allowed at that particular place. He was an intelligent and courteous officer who told them how to get out of the city. Or if they preferred he would show them the way to a hotel. They took the first offer. The officer laughed at their "Tin Lizzie". He was on horseback, which he told them was what he preferred.

We got on the road again, but for once stopped at the first restaurant we got to for a good breakfast. We took it easy that day; we were heading for Detroit and didn't want to get there until the next day.. Detroit was a little out of the way, but we wanted to see the Ford plant. We wanted to see how a car was made and assembled, and Walter wanted to tell them how well the car ws working.

It was almost 10 A.M. when we arrived at the Ford plant. Walter went to the main office. Margit and I stayed in the car. Pretty soon two gentlemen and Walter came out; we were taken on a fine, interesting tour of the Ford factory and assembly plant.

When we got bback to our car we hardly recognized old Lizzy again. They had put new wheels on her, a new windshield, a new top and fenders- she looked real pretty! We were also presented with a couple of pictures of her - "before and after" it said on the envelope. She had a long way to go yet, poor Liz, but we were ready, in great style, for the last leg of our tour.

We headed for Cleveland and from there to Niagara Falls, then down to New York City, where we arrived at Times Square, 42nd and Broadway – six weeks from the day we had left San Francisco.

The magazine Motor had promised recognition and a special medal for anyone driving across the continent that summer. We went to the office; some people came down to our car, where quite a little crowd had gathered. Some took pictures, others wanted to know how the roads were. Walter was presented with the medal for being the first to take that long drive along the Lincoln Highway.

And with that it was all over.

The Model T, developed at
  the Ford Company.

Aka the Tin Lizzie

New York - New Work - New Friends

Walter sold the car; he and Margit went back to California by train. Paul wanted to stay and see New York City and its surroundings

He also had a letter of recommendation from his friend Mr. Farrow, superintendent of Yellowstone National Park, to a friend of his who was a stockbroker. To Paul this was an unfamiliar business; he didn't know a thing about it. But he went to the office and asked for the gentleman whose name was on the envelope.

He was busy, but a man asked me my business and when I told him I was there to buy $100,000 worth of stocks, it seemed like the door to the inner office opened in less time than it would take me to drop off a horse.

I presented my letter to the big boss. He read it and said, "I'll be damned!" Then he asked me if I knew the contents of the letter. I told him no,-- and besides, I didn't have the habit of opening letters belonging to other people. "Well," he growled, "you're in New York now." I couldn't see what difference that made, but he didn't enlighten me, just told me to come back at 2:45 P.M.

When I returned to the office he asked if I was willing to take a position as a long distance courier. I wouldn't require a bond: the letter I had given him took care of that. The first thing I had to do was to make myself ready to go any place I was asked to go. Well, that was easy enough; nobody in particular cared where I went Besides, I wanted to get acquainted with the city and had no intention of staying home, if you can call a room in somebody's apartment "home".

For a few weeks I was in and out of Wall Street and the broker's office. Then I was sent to Chicago with a briefcase full of stock certificates. The case was locked and

*the key evidently sent ahead to a firm in Chicago. I was just told to be careful –
"don't lose it" and "don't let anybody steal it" Beyond that, "long distance" was at
times as far away as Omaha, Nebraska. Once I went to Ogden, Utah.*

*One time I had to wait in Chicago for a week before I again got underway back
to New York. Again I had a full briefcase, locked and sealed. I left on a train from
Chicago about 5 P.M, in a Pullman car, meaning a sleeper. Before I settled for the
night I went to the dining car for a meal. The diner was full, but I was in the front
of the line waiting to get a seat. I was about to meet some very famous people who
made life for me in New York very exciting and interesting.*

Like many other Americans at this time, Paul was an opera fan. The stars of the Metropolitan
Opera toured the country during the off season. Caruso was present in San Francisco at the
time of the earthquake, singing Don Jose in Carmen.. His voice was soon made available
on the records found in the homes of those who owned the first phonograph machines. Paul
was an eager listener to these recordings when he stayed with his friends the Conleys in
Idaho. During his travels he missed no opportunity to hear an opera star singing on stage.
He had never dreamed of a personal encounter with these talented people.

*As I was looking the people over who were eating, my eyes met those of a lady sitting
with two gentlemen. She was evidently looking me over too because she spoke to
the head waiter, who came up to me and asked if I would be good enough to go and
speak with the lady. When I did she asked me to sit down and told the waiter to take
my order.*

*Then she said, "We would like to ask you a question. We were discussing whether
a plain ordinary American would recognize any of us three. Do you know who
we are?"*

*"Yes," I answered. "I do know you, but I must tell you that I am not what you would
call an "ordinary American." That made the lady laugh. "But what are you? – A
prince from Europe?"*

*"No, I am an American, and I am proud of that. And yes, I am plain –I know that..
But I am not ordinary." I then told them my name and called each of them by the
right name – Mr. Martinelli, Mr. Caruso and Madame Tetrazini. They were all opera*

stars from the Metropolitan Opera House. The three of them became my best friends in New York City for the next year.

Paul's new friends encouraged him to quit his job. They gave him all the tickets he wanted for the opera. They introduced him to more opera people than he could possibly wish for.

Once at a very lavish party, with about forty people present, I was appointed "master of ceremonies" – "because," said Giovanni Martinelli, "you can smile but not sing." "And because," said Enrico Caruso, "you can speak such bad Italian, – "bad enough to make anyone laugh or cry."

Far away, on the other side of the "big pond," just as Eski had told him years ago in Idaho, the first world war had begun. Without an American army of sufficient size, Americans were asked to volunteer and all eligible men signed up for the draft. Recalling the words of his Indian friend, Paul was ready and waiting to be drafted.

How did he make a living that year while he was waiting for Uncle Sam to invite him to participate in the war? For a personable young man with much hotel experience it was easy. His first job was at the Waldorf Astoria.

Once I took a room service order up to a lady who turned out to be Madame Schumann-Heink of the Metropolitan. She knew me, of course, and told me she liked me very much. She would like to adopt me. I said, "No, thank you."

"What could I do for you instead?" she asked. – "Would you sing Brahm's lullabye for me?" And she did.

Another one of his friends from the opera wanted Paul to come to the Biltmore, where she was staying. So he went there. Never once did any of the stars let on that they knew him outside of the hotel. That was the way he wanted it.

I had a little fun with Mr. Caruso and Mr. Martinelli once. They had asked me where I lived and I told them "near by – by cab five minutes." One evening around 2A.M. after the opera and supper at the Biltmore, they asked if they could go along home with me. I said okay.

We went by cab to the corner of 3rd Avenue and 37th Street. We got off there and told the cab to wait. We then walked to the middle of the block to a four-story apartment house and started to walk up four flights of stairs. In the corridors were dozens of sewing machines run by children from 8 to 14 years of age – at 2 o'clock in the morning. My friends couldn't believe their eyes.

"This is America?" they said, "Let's go home!" I warned them not to give the kids money. They wouldn't like it. Downstairs they asked again, "You live here?" – "I do, but I don't like it." No more was said about that.

Paul Hansen and Giovanni Martinelli found their own way of providing a bit of help for some of the tenement residents. They would go to the nearest cafeteria and load their trays with far more than anyone could possibly eat. Then they would bag up their "leftovers" and take them back to the tenement. "Say, could you help us out? "they would ask a few of the women. "Our eyes were bigger than our appetites at the cafeteria. We don't know what to do with all this stuff. Could you take it off our hands?"

It was a good kind of fun for every one concerned.

In the Spring of 1918 I went to Atlantic City for a "vacation", which meant I had grown tired of the life in New York City. Walking on the boardwalk, taking in the sights and enjoying some fresh ocean breezes, I passed a Child's Restaurant. Behind the plate glass window I noticed a girl making hot cakes on a large grill. There was a sign in the window stating "Young neat man wanted to work on making hot cakes." Here we go again, I thought, – something new, something different. – I got the job and started in right away. That is how it was everywhere in the USA – not many questions asked. You do the work all right – okay. You are no good at the work – out you go.

Paul liked Atlantic City and the new job as a hot cake maker. He had hardly got round to writing his friends in New York City to tell them about what had become of him, than he was faced with a new change. The latest news about the war in Europe was in the newspaper he was reading while he sat on a bench on the boardwalk. With the entry of the United States into the armed conflict, thousands of American men were being called up to join the American Expeditionary Forces in France. The words of his Indian friend Eski, in Idaho, resounded in his memory across the years. "You will go to fight in a big war. You will go over a very big pond – many days to cross."

On the front page, the newspaper Paul had in his hands posted the number drawn the day before in the draft. Right there in print, big as a house, it seemed to him, was his number. He was sure there was a greeting from Uncle Sam at his address in New York City. Sure enough, there it was waiting for him when he arrived there the next day.

Eski's Prophecies Are Fulfilled

You're in the Army Now

Paul's day for active service in the U.S Army arrived. He had been with his sister and her husband in Brooklyn the evening before. He was to report at 6:00 A.M. near 2nd avenue Eastside at 32nd street. When he arrived, a bit late, there seemed to be a banquet going on in the street. Actually breakfast was being served to anyone who wanted it.. There was singing and music; nobody seemed to be downhearted.

> *About 7:30 I had the pleasure of seeing four members of the Metropolitan Opera arrive and hear them give us some wonderful Arias. How in the world those people got up that early and who told them about the departure that morning I never did find out. I knew all four and told them goodbye in Italian, but they were "dead pan" –just laughed and treated us all alike. I liked that!*

> *Tammany Hall was well represented, gave us both cigars and cigarettes and chewing tobacco. I liked to chew when I was alone. All in all it was a great farewell, not at all like we were off for war.*

After all the big doings on the eastside of New York City, the men went by Fifth Avenue buses and on to the ferry across the Hudson River to the New Jersey side, and then by train to Camp Wadsworth, South Carolina. The training at the army camp was not impressive. They learned how to march and how to take care of their rifles. The sergeant soon discovered that Paul knew how to shoot and gave him something else to do while the rest practiced easy target shooting.

We were eight persons to each tent, which were all there was there when I came. I had not yet got around to taking life too seriously, even soldier life. I found out I had better mend my ways and be quick about it. Once after lunch the eight of us were taking it easy when I proposed an ice cream cone. Nobody else wanted to go to the canteen for them., so I went. On the way back, across a field, I met an officer. Since I had our cones in each hand, I just hollered, "Hello there!" This was not the proper way to salute. The officer called out, "Here, soldier." I went over to him. He said, "You know how to salute?" –"Yes, sir." – "Let me see." PLUNK. There went the eight ice cream cones and I stood "stiff as starch, like an Irishman on the 17th of March." I got a big laugh, as seven other soldiers were watching. No ice cream that day.

Later on, Paul found out more about a soldier's life in Spartanburg, the nearest city.. A group of men wanted to go there for a good dinner. The sergeant at headquarters gave them a strange look when they asked for a pass, but never said a word. He knew they were going to Spartanburg and so would miss their dinner at the camp,. What he didn't tell them was that no enlisted man, meaning a private, rear rank or first class, in the United States Army would be served in any restaurant, south, north, east or west in the U.S.A.

Otherwise we got along fine down in South Carolina. I am not sure what we were supposed to learn, but evidently we must have been good enough to die for our country because there came a day when we were issued a lot of different things. We were told what it was all for and then we packed or rolled it up and expected to have to do it all again. But in a little while we heard the now-familiar order "fall in" and well, well we really did get on army trucks and roll off to the train and back to New Jersey to Camp Merritt where we were to stay till orders came to go to France.

Paul immediately asked for a pass to go to New York City, not really expecting to get it, but was surprised to find it easier than anticipated to get a pass. The pass had no time limit, which, of course, was a slip on the part of the clerk. Paul took advantage of it and didn't return for six days.

I got back ten minutes before we left for the boat that took us to the army transport. Some kind soul had expected me back in time, had packed my belongings and rolled my pack. We also carried a blue sack full of blankets and things and this kind soul (I suspected the sergeant) had filled my sack with 50 pounds of rocks. I didn't know this until we emptied the sacks in the transport. I carried the blooming thing way down below deck to 4F

It was very good down there until we got out on the ocean in a terrific storm. It seemed to me that out of 6000 army boys the 5999 were seasick. The one of the 6000 who didn't get sick was none other than myself.

On the second day out Paul succeeded in getting to the top deck, probably to a section of the boat reserved for sailors only. It was nice and clean up there, especially after escaping the mess down below. It was rough for those who were seasick, but for Paul it was a good crossing. He was by himself, never saw a single person he knew all the way across. Somehow he managed to get three meals a day and slept wherever he could find a place to sleep.

I had the number of my place to sleep down in 4F, but didn't go there until the last night. Then I took the sack, emptied out the rocks, and that made it nice and light to carry

I didn't know a thing about the country we were in, mostly in France, I think, or where we went. All I can say of the war is what was stated on my discharge papers: Battles, engagements, skirmishes, expeditions. AEF Major operations. St. Mihiel Offensive, Sept 12-13, 1918. Minor operations in the Loire, Sept. 1918. Operations between Meuse and Moselle, Sept. 26 – November 11, 1918. Army occupation, November 17, 1918 –July 15, 1919.

I got to know all of my pals during that time – fine fellows. While at camp in South Carolina I started to read the Bible. First I would read it by myself, but pretty soon one or another of the boys would come over and ask, "What are you reading?" After a while we decided I should read aloud half an hour every night. Not one of them had ever read or known the Bible. (Reason: they couldn't read.) After they got used to my English they all liked to hear me read and got to love the stories. Even our hard-boiled sergeant began listening.

In France I got behind with my reading; I was selected for too many special details. When I complained, the sergeant said, "What do you expect, how can I pronounce anybody else's name? Hansen –yes, all right – but Zwichatorsky, Sekorzlwis, Pelniasziko –you try!" I tried and got along real well, but that didn't do me any good. The next night it would be: "I need a couple of volunteers. How about you,

Kramer and Hansen? – "I didn't volunteer," spoke up Kramer. "Neither did I," said Hansen. – "Good," yelled the sergeant. "Let's go, Kramer and Hansen". We gave up and followed the sergeant

I was not a hero –never liked the war. I stuck to my reading whenever I had a chance, so much so that I ended up being called "the evangelist." One cold, snowy morning in Germany we were called out for some kind of review at 9 A.M. A general was to present medals to those who deserved them. When it was all over, some high officers, the general included, came down the lines. They stopped when they got to where I stood., freezing. The general came over to me and asked my name and rank. I gave it with my teeth chattering –. "And what do they call you?" I told him "the evangelist." -- "Do you like medals?" – "No, sir." – "Then," he said, "I'd like to shake your hand. Take your glove off." He took his off and so did I. – "Keep up the good work, and please, no more AWOL" Then he left, but I and 10,000 other freezing doughboys had to stay another 15 minutes.

This gave me time to deal with wondering who had put the general up to this little interruption in the formalities on this frigid day. – It couldn't be anyone but our beloved chaplain, our good old Mormon who had taught me his Articles of Faith, how he believed in being honest and true and being good to all men, even if they took an AWOL once in a great while. That would always remain a great "top secret" for him as long as we would follow the admonition of St. Paul and believe all things and hope all things. We had endured many things and hoped to endure all things. If there was anything virtuous, lovely or of good report, or praiseworthy, we should seek after those things. I would sometimes ask the chaplain if all Mormons took a drink once in a while or smoked cigarettes or ate lots of meat. "Those are words of wisdom," he would answer, "but let's leave it 'Top Secret'."

I didn't care much for duty in the Army of Occupation – 2 hours on, 4 off, so it went all winter, for a while in Coblenz and then out in some small town somewhere along the railroad tracks. When Spring arrived it got better. In our off time we could play baseball; I liked that. We also started getting weekly passes to go to Aix Les Bains, in southern France. It was a fine town and we had rooms and meals in a fine hotel. There was a good YMCA and shows every night

We left Germany without regret, sometime in July, 1919, went to St. Nazaire, and then by transport – a very large boat – back to the good old USA. We were some 8000 on board. It was a good trip across the ocean, no storms at all. We were told there would be a big parade in Boston and we should get everything polished up, including ourselves. As it turned out there was no parade. Before we arrived in Boston harbor some inspectors came on board. We got in line and the inspectors got underway. After twenty minutes they had caught seven cooties –that was too easy. The parade was off. They kept us there for a week, with no visitors allowed —tough on those who had relatives close at' hand. I had none, so it was just another seven days room and board, and wages (a dollar a day for Uncle Sam to pay.)

Paul's mother had sent a courteous letter to General Pershing himself to inquire about whether it might be possible for her son to come for a postwar visit to Denmark before returning to the States. In France he was only a short distance from Koge, where she lived, on the east coast of Denmark.

The general responded with equal courtesy that he was unable to grant her request, since both he and her son must comply with US Army regulations. However he would be able to send an aircraft to fetch and bring her to the port of embarkation, if she were able and willing to accept the offer, so that she might meet with her son before he left for the States.

The lady declined the kind offer, but the letter from General Pershing was given a place of honor in the museum in Koge, where Paul Hansen was born.

The Post War Years and the Totem Pole

Just as his Indian friend, Eski, had said he would, Paul had returned unharmed from the "big war": Walking the familiar streets near 39th and 3rd Avenue, where he had lived for a while in an apartment, he met a man who still lived there.

He told me that they had been keeping a package that came for me It had come about three months before and was wrapped in burlap. Sender: Eski Onez, Idaho. Inside the package I found the beautiful totem pole, some three feet high, that Eski had made for me. With it was a letter, written in Eski's language. I passed it over to the folks in the apartment; they just laughed – couldn't read a word. I did pretty well; I knew Eski's writing and his language.

The letter said: "Welcome home. You now live to be old man, maybe sixty. If you lose totem pole, you get back, but man get killed. Come soon to Idaho; we all like you."

Paul had promised three of his best friends to take care of them while they were in New York City. Now he was able to have them stay with him in his old apartment on the eastside. They stayed for a week, then left for their homes, two of them to California and one to Kentucky. Attempts to stay in touch with them were unsuccessful. The four never saw each other again.

It was August, 1919. I was happy to be out of the army. I found things changed in the USA. For one thing there was now prohibition-- no more saloons or open drinking, like beer or wine with your meals. I didn't approve of it. There was plenty of bootleg drinking going on. I also noticed that women were both smoking and drinking.

Paul stayed in New York for a few years. He tried his hand at selling insurance of various kinds, then got a job as a waiter at a place in Brooklyn called Acme Hall. He could have stayed on there, but he was restless, eager to get back to see his family in Denmark Passage to Europe had not been easy to come by after the war.

In the winter of 1921 I went to the office of the Scandinavian American Line to try and get a ticket to Denmark. While I was standing in line talking to a clerk, Mr. Halvor Jacobsen;, the head of the office, came out. When he saw me he said, "Hello, Mr. Hansen. What are you doing here:?"

I knew him well; he used to work in the San Francisco office. It was time for lunch and he invited me out with him. He was very much interested in all of my doings – we talked a long time.. When it came to getting a ticket to Denmark he couldn't do a thing for me, but he said, "How about taking a job in the first class dining room as steward – just for the crossing?" That was okay with me; he got the captain on the phone and I was hired. I had my passport and was ready to go. A week later I was on a ship heading for Denmark.

Finding a Squaw

I liked the work as a steward and got along fine. The ship was filled to capacity, but the tables in the dining room were far from fully occupied. We had very heavy storms all the way across and only the very bravest of the passengers came for their meals more than once a day. Some of them we never did see in the dining room. They stuck to their cabins and had their meals served there. The storms didn't bother me. All I wanted was to get across.

We got to Copenhagen a few days before Christmas. There was a tremendous crowd on the dock when we arrived, my mother among them. She was the kind of person who was not only loved by her family, but by everyone who ever had the privilege of meeting her. The two of us enjoyed every moment of my homecoming. My mother still lived in Koge, where I was born, about an hour's train ride from Copenhagen. It was good to be there, and to see the family again after so many years.

A Christmas at home – what could be better! There is something about a Danish Christmas I sorely missed in America. I like the way it is all done – the closing of business places in the late afternoon of December 24th, everyone going to church, then the good dinner at home, the lighting of the Christmas tree, the singing and the exchange of gifts – all on Christmas Eve. Christmas Day all is peace and quiet.

My father had passed away while I was in the United States, but some of my brothers and sisters were in Koge for Christmas. After the New Year's celebration, and after having visited my former schoolmates, a few of whom were still in Koge, I thought it would be good to visit some of my family around in Denmark.

I set out by train and boat, and after a few days arrived in Hurup, on the Danish mainland, which is called Jutland. In Hurup there was a gentleman and his family whose name was Stoltze. He was the station master, a respected position in the town. He and his fine wife were in some way related to my family. We always called them uncle and aunt.

I remembered from my childhood days that we children from Koge would take great delight in going for a visit to Uncle Stoltze.. For a while he and his family had lived in Frederickshavn, a coastal town close to Skagen, at the northern tip of Denmark.

There I would quite often go fishing with my uncle. I loved to fish and my uncle also taught me to shoot seals. At that time the seals were a great nuisance, as they had done a great deal of harm to the fishing industry, especially to the herring. We were given two Danish Crowns for each seal we shot. Fishing and hunting at an early age taught me how to handle a gun, and also made me a friend of fishermen, who really had to catch fish for a living.

So here I was, in January 1921, back in Hurup. On the platform waiting for the train was the station t master, Mr. Stoltze, his wife, and a surprise to me – their youngest daughter, Gerda, a sweet-looking young woman. She had been "just a kid" when I was a boy who loved hunting and fishing. I had brought a five-pound box of candy along for my aunt, but I thought better of it. Guess who got the candy? It was love at first sight.

His Indian friend, Eski had advised Paul not to look for his "squaw" in America. She would be found after the war, in which he would take part. He would find her across the "big pond." Paul had recognized her at once when they met.

What was she like this "sweet looking young woman," this Gerda. who had grown from a little girl, one of the many cousins he had seen when he came to visit his aunt and uncle as a boy. She and her brother Knud were the two youngest of those cousins, too young to be of interest to the older boy from Koge who went hunting and fishing with their father.

Their mother, his "tante", loved having children and was creative in finding ways to play with them. In spite of family responsibilities, she and her children had fun together. The older girls learned to share the household duties. Gerda helped her father in the office, tending to train and railroad records and communications. She was quiet, good natured and efficient. When the train bearing her cousin Paul pulled into the station she was close at hand..

Like Paul she knew at once that this man was important, that he meant something very special to her. New emotions filled her heart as she gave him a welcoming smile and clutched the large box of candy that was thrust into her hands. Early on the two acknowledged and shared what they recognized as their mutual attraction and love.

Paul shared colorful accounts of his adventures abroad – of new places and people. Gerda listened, like the other family members, with excited animation. Her own stories were simple tales of life in a family where integrity and responsibility formed the basic texture of everyday life – where love and respect for other human beings were taken for granted.

The basic qualities that life had demanded of them were complementary. Their values and attitudes were harmonious. Each would have something different to give to a marriage. They were both eager to begin a new life together.

It was not long before the two young people were making marriage plans. Before they dared to proceed any further, however, they spoke with the doctor who was Gerda's brother-in-law. Would the physical relationship of the two families obviate the planned marriage? The older man, whose wisdom was known and respected in the family, chuckled quietly. "Your children," he said, will inherit the best of each of your qualities. And that is something you can look forward to and welcome!"

Paul and Gerda decided it would be best if Paul returned to the States to "make a few more dollars" By now he was rather short of cash, and they were both aware of the basic costs involved with setting up housekeeping. It was tough returning to the USA without Gerda. They wrote to each other often, but the two years seemed to go very slowly.

They came to an end at last, and Paul was again ready to depart for Denmark. It was near the end of April, 1923 This time his ticket had been booked well in advance. There was to be no danger of his "missing the boat." The journey took him to Liverpool, then by train to London, with an overnight stay there before proceeding to Harwich. There he boarded the ship that carried him across the North Sea to Denmark The reunion with Gerda, who looked "sweeter than ever" was wonderful. There were two very happy passengers on the train heading north to Hurup.

In Gerda's home they waited, not too patiently, for the wedding day. Plans and preparations had already long since begun, and proceeded cheerfully around them. Inviting fragrances filled the air as the women created those special treats that could be prepared in advance. Speeches were written and new words were composed to familiar songtunes. Song sheets for all the invited guests would be distributed so that all their voices could join in festive celebration of the wedding couple. An enormous "Kransekage" had been ordered from the local baker Composed largely of marzipan, the wedding cake would be made of circles, like wreaths of cake, in graduated diameters, each one a little smaller than the one beneath it, until the tower was topped by the smallest circles of marzipan cake. These might be special souvenirs for the two little girls who would be flower girls at the wedding...Each wreath of the kransekage was festively decorated with white icing.

We were married in good old Danish style in the Lutheran church in Hurup. Gerda looked very very pretty in her beautiful gown. After the church ceremony, we had dinner at Gerda's home. It was a great celebration. There were several kinds of wine, the best food and a very large Kransekage. Some fifty persons were present, including my mother, others of my family and all of Gerda's family and friends. Of course there were songs and speeches, in the best Danish style

After the festivities Gerda and I said a temporary farewell to everyone and went off for a week's stay at a summer resort that was part of a small hotel near the water, some 15 miles from Hurup. It was delightful to have my wife all to myself.. We enjoyed the short honeymoon immensely. The people at the hotel were friends of Gerda and treated us just wonderfully.

Back in Hurup we had a great many people to say goodbye to, but we managed just fine. The day came when we stood on the deck of the steamboat that was to take us to America. "Il ashore that's going ashore." they called out, and we were alone among strangers.

We had the best cabin on the boat, first class, and seats at the captain's table – a long way from my coming to the USA in 1907.

So began our honeymoon in the land of the free and the home of the brave. It became a long honeymoon. We grew old together and were always much in love and very happy.

Finding a squaw...

Gerda

Paul

The wedding guests in Denmark April 1923

Esther and Marie visiting Denmark

Paul's Restaurant in Washington, D.C.

My Father and I

In 1923 Paul E. Hansen once more sailed into the New York harbor. He had come as an immigrant in 1907, as a returning soldier in 1919. Now he came as a husband, bringing with him the woman who would be his faithful partner for the remainder of his long life. I would come to them as their first child; four years later my sister would join us and we would be a family of four.

On their "honeymoon trip" to America, which was ultimately to last indefinitely, Paul was eager to show his wife the wonders of the new world to which they had come. Gerda was thrilled to be a tourist in the city of New York However she could never feel at home there -- that was certain.

Together the new couple weighed the possibilities for the best place to choose as their permanent residence. Paul's friends offered their advice. Washington was the final choice. The capital was a beautiful city, with many trees and parks. The capitol building, the White House, the museums and fine monuments were well worth seeing. The large hotels would afford certain opportunity for the kind of work with which Paul was familiar. The many suburban areas offered surroundings where Gerda would feel at ease, with schools in walking distance for the children they hoped to have some day.

As the first of those children, my name was written on the birth certificate by my father: Esther Egeriis Hansen. The middle name was never used by my father, myself, or my sister. In Denmark, the name had been legally adopted by the family in place of the all-too-common name Hansen. In America Hansen was a name that was easily pronounced and remembered. (as my father was to experience less than enthusiastically during World War I.) The E was retained – a little reminder of the old country.

Two years after their wedding day, on May 20, 1925, my father's mother and one of his sisters came from Denmark to be with us. They found a happy couple, delighted to show off their first child.

It was easy for my father to find work at the Washington Hotel; apartment living in the suburbs of the city provided a setting in which Gerda felt comfortable, trying her way in English with friendly neighbors. They looked forward to celebrating the baby's first Christmas. Soon after that they were anticipating the arrival of a young visitor from Denmark 18-year old Vagn was a quiet boy who lived in close affinity with nature and wanted to learn everything he needed to know to be a good farmer. Now he had been invited to spend a year in Minnesota, where an uncle and aunt had a large farm.

All the arrangements were complete; Christmas 1925 was to be Vagn's last one at home in Denmark, though he faithfully promised to return . .Paul and Gerda had received a letter from him early in December, and had made plans about how best to make his visit with them a happy one.

On the 20th of December back in Denmark Vagn left the farm where he had been working as an apprentice. He took a shortcut across the ice-covered fiord. There was an open hole in the ice, left unmarked by a fisherman. Vagn went through the ice and could not be rescued, although attempts were made. "My grandfather is Stoltze" were his last words, called out to the would-be rescuers.

The tragedy cast a dark shadow over the lives of my young parents at that time. Baby Esther was doubtless a comfort,. but the broken hearted family in Denmark was ever in their thoughts. Gerda mourned especially for Vagn's mother. And Paul felt it only right for his wife to be with her older sister, especially at the time that marked the anniversary of her son's death

My mother and I stayed in Denmark for many months. My father spent that Christmas without his family; his gifts for us, especially for his Esther, signaled his whole-hearted participation. I was already well past my second birthday before he saw us again.

He was a part of my life, close at hand or far away, but always loving, supportive and willing to contribute to my life, in whatever way I might choose to accept or request. Because he loved to write his memoirs. I have been able to include many of his own words in recording the colorful adventures that were part of his life as a young immigrant in the USA..

Now it is my turn to make use of my memories of him as a father, from the time when memories most often begin, at the age of 4, to the time when I was privileged to have him in my home in his nineties, and to be his caregiver.

Childhood Memories

I was four when my sister was born, and for a few days I stayed with friendly strangers who had children. As part of their play I was tucked into a wagon that made a swoosh as it rolled from one side of the street over to the opposite side and up the slanting entryway into the garage.. I felt the movement, heard the sound. With that I came to life. I was awake to being and observing and knowing.-- knowing I was frightened, observing the strange children, not feeling safe until my father came. For me it was the beginning of my childhood memories.

He was all that a child could want or need. With him I knew that I was wanted and needed. He laughed a lot, never cried until I was 7 and had scarlet fever. He was with me in the ambulance that took me to the hospital – I was startled to see him cry. .He gave me love and expressed it in his blue eyes, his protective arms, the kiss on my cheek., his soft Danish words. He knew what to do to make me laugh, to feel secure, to know that the world was full of wonderful things to do, to see and hear, to hold and touch. I knew that I was always safe in his keeping.

When I woke in the morning I might find the results of one of his games, a special favorite that I loved to see. The dolls and toys had been at play during the night! Two of them were dancing with each other, one was riding on the bear-on-wheels. Another was swinging, and still another was turning somersaults. While part of me suspected my father as being the source of all this arrested activity, another part was never quite sure that all the toys had really not been playing while I was asleep. As soon as the sun came up, my father said, the party was over, and every toy had to stop exactly where it was, whatever it was doing. Surely we could all see that they had been playing during the night!

Of course my mother knew how to keep us happy at play. My father worked with her to build a dollhouse where small dolls could live, or a play house that became a center for our own activity. All of us played with a water hose and a small tub in the back yard. One memorable very cold winter he created a skating rink out there. He showed us the best places for sledding on the hills of the neighboring Soldiers Home.

At Christmas my mother taught us all the Danish carols while we baked cookies in the kitchen. It was my father who curtained the living room a few days before Christmas Eve and hung the lights on the tree. He announced firmly that no one was allowed in there until Christmas Eve, when he ceremoniously removed the curtains, after he had lighted the tree. Like the rest of us he adored that special moment when all the other lights were turned off, and the tree became the sudden center of attention. We joined hands and "danced" around the tree. As Caruso himself had once declared, my father was no singer, but he loved to hear the rest of us sing.

Of all his gifts to me, the most precious were our trips to Denmark. It was important, he said, for us to know and be known by our grandparents.

Three times in my childhood, at 6 years old, at 10 and 13 I went with my mother and sister on the journey by ship to Denmark. I was one of that happy crowd of children at the end of May who played together, calling and chatting in English, as the ship moved eastward across the Atlantic. The same group would meet again in September, all of them speaking Danish on the trip back across the ocean to the States.

It was not only the grandparents that I met in Denmark. There were aunts and uncles, and always cousins of the right age to be our chosen playmates. We swam in the North Sea, picked berries from the low-lying bushes that grew among the heather-covered hills of Jutland. One memorable time we attended the festivities at Rebild, the Danish American National Park, likewise located in those hills. In Copenhagen we begged to be taken "just one more time" to Tivoli, that extraordinary amusement park, not only for the rides – the merry go round that my little sister adored -- but for lakes and flowers, music of all sorts, and the theatre with Harlequin and Columbine, and the irresistible Pierrot, who never spoke but was repeatedly implored to "say something, Pierrot!"

Most important, however, were the relationships we established with some of the family members in Denmark. My cousin Rigmor was 13 years older than I, but we became fast friends for life. She was a teacher, as I had always planned to be since I was 5 years old. There were others who also became dear to me. I was honored later in life, to become the godmother of the daughter of one of my cousins.

Thanks to my father we developed a love for Denmark and the Danish people. What we experienced with the family was also a general observation: There was in Denmark a basic integrity, a respect for others, an ability to enjoy life and appreciate modest pleasures.

My Father's Restaurant

My father's dream of having a restaurant of his own was fulfilled in Washington. It was on Upshur Street, just outside the entrance to the Soldiers Home Our row house was very near by, on Rock Creek Church Road. The home was populated by Spanish American war veterans. It was a large well-kept area with buildings surrounded by trees and lawns. In the summer there were concerts from the bandstand on Saturday evenings.

Thanks to my mother's willing labors on behalf of making the little place a clean and comfortable refuge, there were home cooked specialties from her kitchen like beef or oyster stew,. She and my father also went from house to house in the area gaining permission from the neighbors to serve a glass of beer with the meals. This was no problem for my gregarious father, but I realized that it was a particularly courageous effort on my mother's part.

Breakfast was also served in the restaurant. A visitor from Rock Creek Church Road was a botanist associated with the Smithsonian Institution. Her build much resembled that of Mrs. Eleanor Roosevelt, the president's wife.. One day when she had left after enjoying her meal, my father called for attention from the other breakfasters. "I want to ask you please to take care with the language you use in the presence of a distinguished person who has chosen to come here for breakfast." There was a brief silence, followed by a buzz of conversation. The next day when the botanist entered for breakfast, all the old gentlemen rose to their feet, and remained standing until she was seated. Later she asked my father, "Mr Hansen, why did everybody stand up when I came in this morning?." -- "Oh, replied my father, "It was just a sign of respect for a lady."

For a short time, my father kept in the restaurant the totem pole that Eski had made for him It was an admired conversation piece. One day, a man took it off the wall, concealed it under his overcoat and walked as far as just across the street from the restaurant. There he was struck by a car; the totem pole fell to the ground beside him and he fell over -- dead. He had only managed to blurt out, "Take that thing back to Mr. Hansen."

My father remembered what Eski had told him, that the pole would always come back to him if it should be stolen, and that "man get killed." who tried to take it. The totem pole went back to our home. There were to be no more disastrous accidents!

In his memoirs my father warmly endorsed the help and support of his lifetime partner in establishing and maintaining the restaurant. For several years she was not only the cook, but also the manager of the small establishment, and later the ice cream parlor on the opposite side of Upshur Street. This enabled him to retain his job as a waiter at the Washington Hotel. By united efforts they survived the tough years of the depression and even funded vacations along the Atlantic Coast or Chesapeake Bay, and also in Denmark.

I never served as a waitress in the restaurant. My father did not think that to be appropriate for a girl at the time, although later he did employ waitresses and a good cook to take over what had been my mother's steady job.

Personal Help from my Father

I could count on my father's happy pride in my successes, and his lively interest and support in anything I chose to do He was glad when I was qualified, after graduation from the teachers college, to teach in the D.C. Public Schools. I became a teacher in the middle grades at Stuart Junior High School. I still lived with my parents at that time, but was earning real money, and was able to pay my own way for the trip to Denmark with my mother and sister in 1947.

It was a glorious summer. Two summers after the five grim years of Nazi occupation the Danes were able to enjoy several months of unusually warm, sunny weather. We joined in endless picnics and parties; we were the focal point of repeated celebrations as we traveled about the country to the scattered members of my mother's family. There was wonderful swimming and boating in the blue fiords and endless conversations to catch up with the lost news of numerous years.

For me, the best conversations were with my cousin Rigmor We talked over the dishwashing in the kitchen, resumed our talk stretched out on grassy places under the beech trees or sitting among the wildflowers in country ditches.

For the first time I had found someone who could answer my questions. Oh yes, I was a teacher; I knew how to respond to the innumerable questions that schoolchildren ask. But I had yet to hear believable responses to my own questions. The Lutheran pastor himself and the young assistant pastors endeavored to enlighten us. I had never felt enlightened. The things they earnestly accepted as truth did not engage my belief. They could not answer my questions.

My cousin Rigmor could. What she told me I knew to be true. It made me feel completely alive and awake. Filled with joy and wonder I began to plan for the future. I was an adult. I could make decisions for myself. What was I to do now? It was not enough to say simply "I want to stay in Europe."

Rigmor was able to help me define and justify my feelings and render them into reasonable goals. As a French teacher I could profit from spending time studying in a French speaking country. If I was to give up my position in the D.C. public schools I must present my views in acceptable terms for those in authority.

I gained admission to the University of Neuchatel in Switzerland. I wrote letters to those in charge of education in the schools where I had previously taught. And I sent copies of this correspondence to my father in Washington.

His response was prompt and definite. He wrote in a telegram these words, which I have kept preserved in a scrapbook of pictures from that very special time of my life.

> YOUR LETTER TO CANTRELL SPLENDID. STAY IN EUROPE.. I LIKE YOUR IDEAS. SEE YOU NEXT MAY. GOOD LUCK. FATHER

On the same page in my scrapbook of memoirs I included a copy of Robert 'Frost's poem "The Road Not Taken", ending with these words:

> Two roads diverged in a wood and I –
> I took the one less traveled by,
> And that has made all the difference.

Following that telegram came a check for $1000, a great deal of money in 1947.

I have been grateful all my life for my father's support, which helped significantly in bringing about that difference.

My Father's Life and Mine: Our Separate Ways Together and Apart

I came home from Europe in May to help with the festive celebration of my parents' silver wedding anniversary,. Soon after that came my sister's wedding – again with songs and speeches, always with my father's the best of them.

At 65 he retired and marked the day in his own way, by giving up smoking. It was an important step in combating the effects of asthma, bronchitis and emphysema. These and other ills presented significant problems during his life; they included a retinal detachment that cost the loss of his left eye; he also had a hearing loss. Yet he never complained, and never tired of giving speeches.

I was still for a time actively involved in the life of my parents and the family as a whole. My friend Mascha, a refugee from Hitler's desecrations who had lost, in Germany, all those who were dear to her, came to live in Washington. She was welcomed in my family home where she formed a special relationship with my father, with whom she became best able to speak of the unspeakable things she had experienced.

In retirement both of my parents were eager to travel, and glad to escape the humid heat of Washington. The Poconos, the Catskills and Lake Placid were among the nearby favorites. They also visited my sister in Canada and met their first grandchild. A second child followed and a third was on the way when the parents separated.

With two young children and expecting a third my sister returned to her old home on Rock Creek Church Road in Washington. The welcome mat was out for them. Paul and Gerda became active grandparents. I loved being an aunt to the two older children and the new baby For a time we managed the practical and emotional demands of being a family of seven.

The decision to divide into separate living quarters, at first in D.C. and later in nearby Maryland was best for all of us. A working mom with three children, a teacher-aunt and grandparents all within walking distance of each other worked out well. I was able to offer my services as a sitter regularly or from time to time for the children, as did my parents. They were more able now to enjoy the peace and quiet of retirement.;

Again they were also able to travel, far more extensively in the States, and to Europe as well. Trips brought them not only to Denmark, but to France, Belgium, Italy, Germany and Austria. They were reunited with friends and family, made new friends, met with people who had become important to me and to whom I was glad to send them with my personal introduction.

My Father and I in Arizona

When my father was advised by his physician that a climate change would improve his well- being and prolong his life I had little doubt about what his choice would be. While he yearned for the long-loved mountains of Colorado, he knew he could not tolerate or survive the altitude there. His grandchildren were now with their mother in Tucson, Arizona. It was the right choice for him.

It became the choice for me. I made a trip to Tucson, found and purchased a house that could pleasantly accommodate the three of us. I knew that both of my parents would soon require a live-in caregiver. I would be that person. I could tutor children in the home and still make myself available as much as might be needed. A car would be essential for our convenience, and our freedom. It was high time I learned to drive!

Learning how best to cope with life in an unfamiliar environment is not easy for the elderly. As I struggled with trying to create a satisfactory professional life for myself, I helped, as best I could with practical problems. Both of my parents had increasingly challenging health conditions. I took driving lessons, I gave up the fellowship I had been offered at the University of Arizona, I developed my own program to serve the needs of disabled readers. I found and joined a support group for people like me. And I became a caregiver.

Some of the particulars of that role are presented in the book that I wrote later to offer support to those who find themselves in similar circumstances. The book is called *A Matter of Growth* It has been gratefully received by many. The title was apt. We lived, we struggled, and each of us grew in our different ways. There are pages in the book dedicated to my father, especially during the last days, before he left his physical body.

In this book, with the focus on my father, it has been easy to tell of his life from the time he came to this country as a 21-year old to his departure at the age of 94. It has been fun to describe his adventures, in part through the use of his own memoirs. I have depicted him as the less-than-ordinary man he was, happy in adventuring and in relationships with many persons of high and low estate. I have told of his wonder and veneration for nature,. his love for his family, his willingness to work, and always to give, in whatever form might be right for the moment at hand.

Of his thoughts, his meditations, my father seldom if ever spoke. I knew, from what he wrote, that he had the habit of going into empty churches at the end of his work day. There, it would seem, he practiced quiet personal introspection; he did not exchange thoughts with others. He adopted the habit of reading the Bible and was given the nickname "the evangelist" during the war, because he regularly read the Bible to others who were non-readers. He and the chaplain were good friends; the cleric would answer his young friend's questions about his Mormon beliefs.

My father was not interested in being a Mormon. He was nominally, a Lutheran, as are almost all Danish Christians. As for that, his feelings were perhaps best expressed in the answer he gave to the Episcopalian churchgoer who asked why he, as a Lutheran, was willing to help paint an Episcopal church. My father said, "I'll tell you a secret. God does not know that I am a Lutheran, and if He did, He wouldn't care." He would go to church if there was a good minister who had something worthwhile to say. Otherwise organized religion did not appeal to him.

Talking with ministers was something my father liked to do. In Canada, he and the bishop of the area in which his married daughter lived, enjoyed each other's company.. In Washington, he invited the Danish pastor for dinner and liked talking with him. His memoirs record the names of his favorite pastors at Luther Place Memorial Church in Washington They would also come for a meal at our house from time to time. Once he had the restaurant, my father was too busy to go to church. His wife, however, was active in the women's groups, and my father enjoyed a hearty chuckle over becoming known as "Mrs Hansen's husband.".

A prayer of thanksgiving was deeply embedded in my father's memory. He told me once of an experience he had during the first World War. With a buddy he had been trapped in a shell hole for thirty hours. Their only food was hardtack. As they broke this bread together they joined in giving thanks. The words of that prayer remained with him and seemed to re-echo in prayers spoken at other times and places. Later he tried to locate that buddy, for he felt that the man had knowledge he wanted to share. However he never saw him again.

In his travels, he wanted to go, with my mother, to the place where friends of mine lived. With them he heard what seemed to him an accurate reflection of the prayer of thanksgiving he had heard years ago on the battlefield in France. He recorded it in his memoirs: "O Lord, in the weaving of thy creation, thou hast graciously spread our table with thine abundance. Accept our thanks for thy goodness." After the prayer, he wrote in his memoirs: "I am alive! I wonder!"

When I spoke, at the table the three of us shared in Arizona, the words I had brought with me from Europe, they had special meaning for my father. There was time now to give more attention to what I had to say. Again, though, he did not give voice to his thoughts. But he read. I left on the front room table my copy of the book *In the Light of Truth – the Grail Message* by Abdrushin. There was a marker in the book. In the course of the days that passed during the remaining few years of his life, the marker moved steadily forward. Of that book my father said, *"It is as clear as the purest spring water."*

When I gave expression to my joy at seeing that he was reading the book, he said only, *"Yes, I know many things, but I do not talk about them. For your mother is not able to go that way"*

In spite of his physical handicaps my father continued his daily walks, and as always, his chats with new people. "Is your father safe?" the people at the bank asked, having seen him on his daily jaunts. A single time I followed him at a safe distance in the car. That excursion proved what I knew to be true: he was safe in the quiet neighborhood, or if the worst were to occur, some stranger he had chatted with before would be quick to help him.

His last days, confined to his bed, were challenging, but not sad. Once quit of the terrifying notion that he was somehow being held prisoner, he recognized both my mother and me. He spoke only Danish, and asked, as he recognized each of us, *"What are you doing here?"*

Waking from a deep sleep, he knew me when I came into his room.

You know," he said, *"I have been in the other world, and they were all there." And they said to me, 'We know Esther; she is a good person. Give her our greetings ' So if you want a greeting from the other side, I can give you one."* And he held out his hand. *"And they said to me that I had to go back to this world, but that I would be a different person; I would eat only a little bit. But soon I would be able to come back to them."*

Another day, he stirred as I entered. "Are you there?" "Yes."

"It might happen that you come back and they tell you that your father is dead. But don't let that bother you." 'No, for we'll find each other again." *Very firmly, he responded, "Yes, for all who have loved one another come together again."* "Yes, they do."

There were days when he was uncertain of our identity, when he wanted to pay us for helping him. At other times he was quite lucid: I would assert my love for him. Once he said: *"I love you more than I can ever say."*

About his memoirs he stated clearly, *"If I have written anything negative about anyone in my memoirs, cross it out. We all make mistakes."*

He often repeated his thanks, always in Danish*: "Tak for idag." – Thank you for today. Thank you all of you. Thank you for this year."*

Often we sang old Danish folk songs to him, or we played the beautiful tapes of Danish songs sung by Aksel Schiotz. On the next-to-last night I played for him the sound of bells ringing from a bell tower over the Tirolean Alps, along with music for worship. My father was quiet, totally at peace.

With his wife beside him on the last night he asked, as he had before, *"When are we going home?"* The next day he was on his way.

He is remembered by those who knew him as Mr. Hansen, Paul, Uncle Paul and Popsy. He was friend, husband, father, grandfather and even great grandfather to two who were little boys at the time – one of them born just four days before his passing on the first of December, 1980..

We recall the story of his meeting with the Metropolitan Opera stars who wished to know if "just a plain ordinary American" would recognize and be able to identify them. That was no problem for an ardent opera fan. But he wrote in his memoirs: "I passed their test, but they failed completely because I'm not a plain, ordinary American -- American – yes! Plain – yes, but Ordinary – No!"

We know he was not an ordinary man. We could well wish that a great number of "ordinary men" were more like what he was.

About the Author

Esther E Hansen was born in Washington, D.C. where she attended the Teachers College, began her teaching career, and later worked with the Kingsbury Center.When she moved with her parents to the southwest, professional relationships helped her to establish Tucson Educational Services, which became an important asset in the community.She developed a valued staff of tutors whom she trained to make use of the skills she herself continued to use in her own teaching of disabled readers.

On retirement she chose to settle in central Ohio in an area of farmland and beautiful wooded hillsides. In the village of Gambier she has friends close at hand as well as the many cultural benefits available to the public through nearby Kenyon College.

In the natural impulse to share the life experiences which may be of value to others she has written , in addition to her father's story, two other books: *A Matter of Growth* was inspired by her life as a caregiver with her parents, and *90 Years Young* tells of her many adventures with wellness.

Printed in the United States
By Bookmasters